DATE DUE

DEADLY DISEASES AND EPIDEMICS

INFLUENZA

Second Edition

Antibiotic-resistant
  Bacteria

Anthrax, Second Edition

Avian Flu

Botulism

Campylobacteriosis

Cervical Cancer

Cholera, Second Edition

Dengue Fever and
  Other Hemorrhagic
  Viruses

Ebola

Encephalitis

Escherichia coli
  Infections

Gonorrhea

Hantavirus Pulmonary
  Syndrome

Helicobacter pylori

Hepatitis

Herpes

HIV/AIDS

Infectious Diseases of
  the Mouth

Infectious Fungi

Influenza,
  Second Edition

Legionnaires' Disease

Leprosy

Lung Cancer

Lyme Disease

Mad Cow Disease
  (Bovine Spongiform
  Encephalopathy)

Malaria

Meningitis

Mononucleosis,
  Second Edition

Pelvic Inflammatory
  Disease

Plague

Polio

Prostate Cancer

Rabies

Rocky Mountain
  Spotted Fever

Salmonella

SARS

Smallpox

Staphylococcus aureus
  Infections

Streptococcus (Group A)

Streptococcus (Group B)

Syphilis

Tetanus

Toxic Shock Syndrome

Trypanosomiasis

Tuberculosis

Tularemia

Typhoid Fever

West Nile Virus

DEADLY DISEASES AND EPIDEMICS

INFLUENZA

Second Edition

Donald Emmeluth, Ed.D.

CONSULTING EDITOR
Hilary Babcock, M.D., M.P.H.,
Infectious Diseases Division,
Washington University School of Medicine,
Medical Director of Occupational Health (Infectious Diseases),
Barnes-Jewish Hospital and St. Louis Children's Hospital

FOREWORD BY
David Heymann
World Health Organization

CHELSEA HOUSE
PUBLISHERS
An imprint of Infobase Publishing

Chelsea House
An imprint of Infobase Publishing
132 West 31st Street
New York, NY 10001

Library of Congress Cataloging-in-Publication Data
Emmeluth, Donald.
  Influenza / Donald Emmeluth ; foreword by David Heymann, World Health Organization. -- 2nd ed.
      p. cm. -- (Deadly diseases and epidemics)
  Includes bibliographical references and index.
  ISBN-13: 978-1-60413-236-6 (alk. paper)
  ISBN-10: 1-60413-236-1 (alk. paper)
  1. Influenza--Juvenile literature. I. Title.
  RC150.E466 2008
  616.2'03--dc22
                                    2008028100

Chelsea House books are available at special discounts when purchased in bulk quantities for businesses, associations, institutions, or sales promotions. Please call our Special Sales Department in New York at (212) 967-8800 or (800) 322-8755.

You can find Chelsea House on the World Wide Web at http://www.chelseahouse.com

Series design by Terry Mallon
Cover design by Takeshi Takahashi

Printed in the United States of America

Bang EJB 10 9 8 7 6 5 4 3 2 1

This book is printed on acid-free paper.

All links and Web addresses were checked and verified to be correct at the time of publication. Because of the dynamic nature of the Web, some addresses and links may have changed since publication and may no longer be valid.

Table of Contents

Foreword

Communicable diseases kill and cause long-term disability. The microbial agents that cause them are dynamic, changeable, and resilient: they are responsible for more than 14 million deaths each year, mainly in developing countries.

Approximately 46 percent of all deaths in the developing world are due to communicable diseases, and almost 90 percent of these deaths are from AIDS, tuberculosis, malaria, and acute diarrheal and respiratory infections of children. In addition to causing great human suffering, these high-mortality communicable diseases have become major obstacles to economic development. They are a challenge to control either because of the lack of effective vaccines, or because the drugs that are used to treat them are becoming less effective because of antimicrobial drug resistance.

Millions of people, especially those who are poor and living in developing countries, are also at risk from disabling communicable diseases such as polio, leprosy, lymphatic filariasis, and onchocerciasis. In addition to human suffering and permanent disability, these communicable diseases create an economic burden—both on the work force that handicapped persons are unable to join, and on their families and society, upon which they must often depend for economic support.

Finally, the entire world is at risk of the unexpected communicable diseases, those that are called emerging or re-emerging infections. Infection is often unpredictable because risk factors for transmission are not understood, or because it often results from organisms that cross the species barrier from animals to humans. The cause is often viral, such as Ebola and Marburg haemorrhagic fevers and severe acute respiratory syndrome (SARS). In addition to causing human suffering and death, these infections place health workers at great risk and are costly to economies. Infections such as Bovine Spongiform Encephalopathy (BSE) and the associated new human variant of Creutzfeldt-Jakob Disease (vCJD) in Europe, and avian influenza A (H5N1) in Asia, are reminders of the seriousness of emerging and re-emerging infections. In addition, many of these infections have the potential to cause pandemics, which are a constant threat our economies and public health security.

Science has given us vaccines and anti-infective drugs that have helped keep infectious diseases under control. Nothing demonstrates the effectiveness of vaccines better than the successful eradication of smallpox, the decrease in polio as the eradication program continues, and the decrease in measles when routine immunization programs are supplemented by mass vaccination campaigns.

Likewise, the effectiveness of anti-infective drugs is clearly demonstrated through prolonged life or better health in those infected with viral diseases such as AIDS, parasitic infections such as malaria, and bacterial infections such as tuberculosis and pneumococcal pneumonia.

But current research and development is not filling the pipeline for new anti-infective drugs as rapidly as resistance is developing, nor is vaccine development providing vaccines for some of the most common and lethal communicable diseases. At the same time providing people with access to existing anti-infective drugs, vaccines, and goods such as condoms or bed nets—necessary for the control of communicable diseases in many developing countries—remains a great challenge.

Education, experimentation, and the discoveries that grow from them, are the tools needed to combat high mortality infectious diseases, diseases that cause disability, or emerging and re-emerging infectious diseases. At the same time, partnerships between developing and industrialized countries can overcome many of the challenges of access to goods and technologies. This book may inspire its readers to set out on the path of drug and vaccine development, or on the path to discovering better public health technologies by applying our present understanding of the human genome and those of various infectious agents. Readers may likewise be inspired to help ensure wider access to those protective goods and technologies. Such inspiration, with pragmatic action, will keep us on the winning side of the struggle against communicable diseases.

David L. Heymann
Assistant Director General,
Health Security and Environment
Representative of the Director General for Polio Eradication
World Health Organization
Geneva, Switzerland

1

Deadly World Traveler

We live in a time of marvelous medical achievements. Scientists have identified and copied many of our genes and have inserted some of them into bacteria to produce, for example, the insulin that diabetics need. They have even genetically engineered bananas and potatoes so that one day we may be vaccinated while eating them. They have also begun using **viruses** as carriers of genetic information in gene therapy experiments.

In spite of these medical achievements, the Centers for Disease Control and Prevention (CDC) reports that every year more than 36,000 Americans die from **influenza** or as it is commonly known, the flu. In addition, more than 120,000 require hospitalization due to complications of the flu, and thousands more lose valuable time away from work or school. Everyone knows someone who has had the flu.

No one knows when or where influenza began. The Greek physician Hippocrates documented an outbreak of a flulike disease about 412 B.C. in a region that is now part of Turkey. Two hundred years later, the historian Livy described a disease that struck the Roman army that might have been influenza.

Recorded history is unclear as to when the next outbreak of influenza took place. Some evidence suggests that in the late Middle Ages influenza was spread by the Crusaders. Indeed, the name "influenza" was first used about this time. People thought that the disease was caused by some catastrophic or cosmic "influences." Epidemics of disease in Italy in 1357 and 1387 were soon being described as influenza.

During the 1500s, three major outbreaks of influenza occurred in Europe. The outbreak of 1580 probably qualified as a worldwide **epidemic** or **pandemic**. In the 1620s there were reports of influenza in both

Figure 1.1 Martinus Beijerinck, pictured here working in his laboratory, laid the foundation for the study of viruses. In 1899, Beijerinck was investigating tobacco mosaic disease and discovered that a "living fluid," which was not part of the plant itself, was responsible for causing the disease. He hypothesized that other plant diseases could also be caused by a similar agent. (© Lesley A. Robertson for the Delft School of Microbiology Archive, Delft University of Technology, Netherlands)

Virginia and New England, and the first recorded epidemic of influenza in North America occurred in 1647. Historical reports suggest that influenza was present from South Carolina to New England during most of the 1700s. The epidemic of 1759 was particularly devastating to the elderly population. In 1790, President George Washington was struck by influenza, and his own doctor predicted Washington's death. But Washington's fever broke, and he survived. A few months later, Thomas Jefferson and James Madison developed the disease, and Jefferson was said to have suffered with terrible headaches for more than a month. Fortunately, all the leaders of the new nation survived.

This epidemic in the United States was relatively minor compared to the pandemic that had swept through Europe in the early 1780s. Historical records show that two-thirds of the population of Rome and three-fourths of the population of Britain were afflicted with the disease. But so far, no one had any idea of the cause.

During the 1800s, science and technology combined to find answers to many medical questions. Although the causes of many diseases were discovered, the cause of influenza remained unknown. Some physicians believed that a virus could be the cause, especially since our knowledge of viruses was growing at the end of the 1800s. In 1898, two investigators named Friedrich Loeffler and P. Frosch were studying an animal skin disease known as foot-and-mouth disease. They were surprised that the agent of the disease was smaller than bacteria because it was able to pass through filters designed to trap the smallest bacteria. The following year, in 1899, a Dutch microbiologist, Martinus Beijerinck (Figure 1.1), was trying to find the cause of tobacco mosaic disease, a disease that afflicts tobacco plants. He called the agent he found in the sick plants a *contagium vivum fluidum* or contagious living fluid, a name that reflected his uncertainty about the true nature of a virus. This agent ultimately did turn out to be a virus.

Beijerinck recognized that he was dealing with a different form of microbe (minute life form), and he predicted that a similar agent might cause other plant diseases. His insights became the building blocks for the field of **virology**. In 1900, Walter Reed discovered that a virus caused yellow fever in humans. An understanding of the viral basis of many diseases was now becoming clearer. However, it would be another 33 years before scientists saw the influenza virus by using an electron microscope.

As the twentieth century began, the United States was actively pursuing a policy of expansion and becoming more involved in the events in the rest of the world. Economically and politically, the United States was increasing its influence throughout the world. Unfortunately, that expansion would also bring involvement in the Great Influenza Pandemic as travelers spread the virus across the globe.

Influenza arrived on the sunny northern coast of Spain in February 1918. Although the weather was warm, an increasing number of people were sweating not from the heat but from the high fevers associated with the disease. In spite of all the efforts by health officials, the disease spread. Beautiful San Sebastian, Spain, an attractive city and popular tourist destination, was where the first wave of influenza struck. The great pandemic to follow would be known as the **Spanish Flu**. Two months later, it seemed that all of Spain was affected. Historians have suggested that 8 million people, including the king, were ill, although only a few hundred died. Government offices were forced to close, and vehicular traffic came to a standstill. The troops called it the "three-day fever," although the aftereffects lasted at least a week. The Spanish Flu spread throughout Europe, Asia, and the United States. Millions of people in all walks of life were affected.

In 1957, a new strain of influenza virus was isolated in Beijing, China. Some suggested that the disease had started in Russia. In early April, the virus reached Hong Kong after infecting large numbers of people in Singapore and Japan.

The pandemic involved 22 million cases and became known as the **Asian Flu**. Then, in 1968–1969, a new **Hong Kong Flu** claimed 700,000 lives globally. About 34,000 people died in the United States.

In 1976, a new influenza virus was identified in an army recruit at Fort Dix, New Jersey. It was known as the swine flu, and it was feared that this flu was related to the influenza strain of 1918–1919. The government began a massive influenza immunization program. Luckily, the swine flu epidemic never materialized.

Then in 1997, another Hong Kong Flu emerged. Eighteen people became ill, and six died. This flu was unique because it seemed to be carried by chickens and moved directly from chickens to people. To stop the outbreak, more than a million chickens were slaughtered in Hong Kong. Although this seems cruel, it was the smart way to stop a pandemic and was necessary from a public health point of view. When and where will this deadly traveler strike in the twenty-first century? Answers to the questions of where and when this deadly traveler will go have been serious concerns to scientists and the lay public. Given the worldwide access of people and viruses to airline transportation, the spread of new flu viruses has the capability to be swift and far reaching. The spread of influenza viruses does not always follow the conventional wisdom in areas of the world that do not have the traditional seasonal bouts of influenza. For example, in the southern hemisphere and in tropical areas, influenza has been found to travel from areas of low population into the populated areas; in the northern hemisphere flu tends to move from populated areas to less densely populated areas.

In a study done in Brazil, the researchers found that viruses did not spread from the highest population density regions into other regions. Instead, the movement was from the low population density regions around the equator into the more populous regions of the south of Brazil. Some of the reasons for

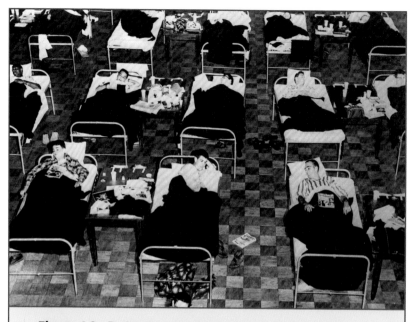

Figure 1.2 During the second half of the twentieth century, Asian Flu claimed the lives of more than 700,000 people around the world. The epidemic was so severe that colleges set up temporary infirmaries to house the patients, such as this one in the ballroom at the University of Massachusetts. (© Bettmann/Corbis)

this may be temperature related. The importance of the study relates to the fact that little is known about the circulation of the influenza viruses at these latitudes. It is important to understand how to determine the composition of the flu vaccines and to be able to provide guidance to identify the appropriate time of administering that vaccine.[1]

As we move into the twenty-first century, there has been an increase in deaths of various types of fowl, leading to this era being known as the time of "bird flu." We will explore this type of influenza in a later chapter and explain why people are concerned that it could lead to a pandemic more deadly than any previously mentioned.

2

What Is a Virus?

Viruses have always been difficult to define. The Dutch microbiologist Beijerinck thought the disease agent he called a virus was a contagious, living fluid. *Virus* comes from the Latin word meaning "slimy, poisonous, liquid." By the 1500s it referred to the venom of snakes, and the term was eventually adopted by the medical community to describe the spread of some diseases. By 1908, scientists knew that viruses could cause diseases of plants, animals, and even humans. By 1940, scientists were taking pictures of viruses through the transmission electron microscope, a microscope using electrons rather than visible light to produce magnified images. What is a virus? Is it like a cell?

For something to be considered a cell, three criteria must be met. First, there needs to be a membrane serving as a boundary for the structure. Second, a fluid environment must exist in which biochemical reactions occur; this is surrounded by the membrane. Third, the cell must contain genetic information in the form of DNA. The DNA is arranged into one or more chromosomes and contains the information codes for the cell. **Eukaryotic** cells, such as plants, animals, fungi, and **protists** whose cells contain a distinct membrane-bound nucleus, may have additional **organelles** inside the fluid environment. Protists are organisms that are, with few exceptions, microscopic. They are divided into three subgroups: protozoa, algae, and fungal-like water molds and slime molds. **Prokaryotic** cells such as bacteria, which do not contain a distinct membrane-bound nucleus, do not have additional organelles. Does a virus meet the criteria for being a cell? If a virus does not qualify as a cell, it cannot be considered alive. The cell theory tells us that all living things are composed of one or more cells. The cell is the basic unit of life. Therefore, if a virus does not qualify as a cell, can we consider it a living thing? Can we call it an organism? Before these questions can be answered a look at the structure of a typical virus and then the structure of the influenza virus is necessary.

VIRAL BASICS

The structural parts that make up a virus have been known since the 1930s. Viruses continue to surprise us with their diversity and their unique solutions to the problems of survival. A virus contains a single type of nucleic acid, either DNA or RNA. It cannot contain both. The DNA or RNA may be double-stranded or single-stranded. This core of nucleic acid is known as the viral **genome** and is covered by a protein coat called a **capsid**. The genetic information in the DNA or RNA contains the codes for producing and assembling more viruses. The capsid is composed of protein subunits called **capsomeres**. Viruses that consist only of a capsid and a nucleic acid are called **nucleocapsids**, or naked viruses.

Some viruses have an additional outer covering called an **envelope**. The envelope is composed of phospholipids and glycoproteins in most viruses. Cell membranes consist of phospholipids and glycoproteins, too. Phospholipids are molecules made by combining phosphate groups (H_2PO_4) with different types of fatty acids. Glycoproteins are combinations of simple sugars and proteins. (The prefix "glyco" refers to sugars). As new virus particles are being assembled and finally leave their host cell, or the cell that houses them, they take some of the host cell membrane materials with them. The virus may also add some of its own glycoproteins to the envelope. Some of these may appear as spikes. A virus with an envelope, with or without spikes, is called an enveloped virus.

As can be seen, viruses lack the structures that we normally associate with cells. In addition, viruses have no metabolic machinery of their own. They cannot carry out any of the functions we associate with living things unless they are inside a host cell. Viruses use the raw materials and the metabolic machinery of their host to direct the production and assembly of new viruses. One could consider a virus an **intracellular parasite**. Since viruses depend on their host cells for replication (making exact copies of themselves), they can be difficult to grow in the laboratory. In order to do research and testing on viruses, scientists must grow the viruses in animal cells, such as chicken eggs.

STRUCTURE OF THE INFLUENZA VIRUS

The influenza virus is an enveloped virus. This envelope is composed mainly of a lipid bilayer and is lined with a type of protein known as the matrix protein. This combination of lipids and protein is sometimes called the matrix protein membrane. The outer surface is covered with two types of spikes made of glycoproteins and embedded in the envelope. The first type is known as **hemagglutinin**, abbreviated as HA. The name refers to the fact that the influenza virus can attach itself to red blood cells and cause them to clump or agglutinate. This same HA glycoprotein is responsible for the attachment of the virus to the host cell and for beginning the process of infecting the cell. The second type of glycoprotein spike is called **neuraminidase**, or NA. The "-ase" ending on its name indicates that it is an **enzyme**. NA's major job seems to be allowing the newly formed viruses to leave the host cell without sticking to each other or the host cell. There are about four to five times more HA proteins than NA proteins in the lipid envelope.

There are three **types** of influenza viruses. Type A contains many **subtypes** and has been the major culprit in causing epidemics and pandemics in the last 100 years. Type B has been responsible for some regional level epidemics. Type C seldom creates major problems and is found only in humans. Neither type B nor type C has any known subtypes. Differences in the three types of viruses are caused by differences in the HA and NA proteins, the viral genetic information the virus contains, and the matrix protein.

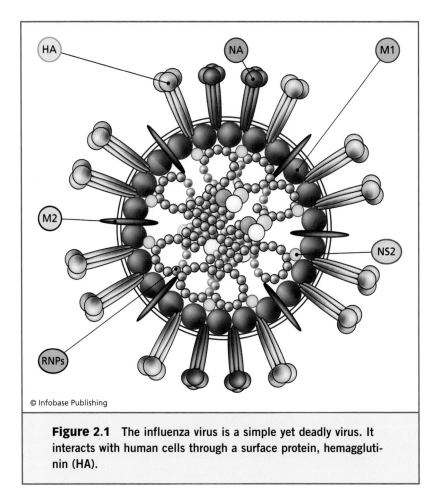

© Infobase Publishing

Figure 2.1 The influenza virus is a simple yet deadly virus. It interacts with human cells through a surface protein, hemagglutinin (HA).

INFLUENZA GENOMES

The influenza genomes for types A and B influenza virus consist of eight separate, single-stranded RNA segments containing 10 genes. Type C contains only seven RNA segments. These RNA segments are coated by helical or spiral nucleoproteins creating segments sometimes known as ribonucleoproteins (RNPs). Recall that this combination of genome and protein covering is also known as the nucleocapsid. The nucleocapsid of influenza viruses is surrounded by an envelope. Each of

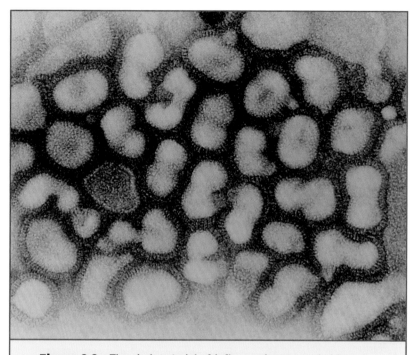

Figure 2.2   The viral material of influenza is surrounded by a special protein coat. The coat is covered by a lipid layer. Notice the spikes on the outer surface of the coat, or envelope, of the influenza type A culture in this picture. (Courtesy CDC/Dr. Erskine Palmer)

the RNA segments has the code for one or more of the viral proteins. Table 2.1 provides the current understanding of the influenza virus genes and their functions. The influenza virus is one of very few viruses to have its genome in separate segments. This segmenting of the genome increases the likelihood that new genetic sequences will develop if two different strains of virus infect a cell at the same time. Gene segments from each of the strains may produce new combinations leading to a new strain of flu. On the positive side, laboratory duplication of the genome segments may lead to new **vaccine** strains to inoculate people against these viral strains.

Table 2.1 Genes of Influenza A and Their Presumed Functions

#1	PB2 gene	Codes for an RNA polymerase involved in cap binding (sealing end of molecule); part of transcriptase, which is an enzyme that converts DNA into types of RNA
#2	PB1	Codes for an RNA polymerase involved in elongation of the molecule; part of transcriptase
#3	PA gene	Codes for an RNA polymerase that may serve as a protease; part of transcriptase
#4	HA gene	Codes for hemagglutinin; at least five distinct hemagglutinins are found in human infections (H1, H2, H3); others have been found in animal flu viruses
#5	NP gene	Codes for the nucleoproteins; types A, B, and C have different nucleoproteins; part of transcriptase complex
#6	NA gene	Codes for neuraminidase; involved with release of virus from the host cell; two different neuraminidases have been found in human viruses (N1,N2); at least seven others in other animals, e.g., chickens, pigs, ducks
#7	M1 gene M2 gene	Matrix protein; different sections of the genetic code of the gene are read to produce the two proteins that open channels in the cell membrane and allow charged atoms or molecules (ions) to pass through
#8	NS1 gene NS2 gene	Codes for two different nonstructural proteins whose function is still unknown; as above, different sections of the code are used for each

In 2006, a team from the National Institute of Arthritis and Musculoskeletal and Skin Disease (NIAMS) was able to produce an image of one of the viruses that cause influenza. The group worked with a seasonal strain of the virus known as H3N2. They were able to distinguish different kinds of virus particles in their sample and to look at the distribution of the molecules in each of the different kinds. Using a technique called cryoelectron tomography, they were able to picture the three-dimensional structure of more than 100 individual variants of the H3N2 strain of influenza A. Their pictures were able to determine differences in the hemagglutinin glycoproteins and neuraminidase proteins in the viral covering. They were also able to figure out the makeup of the protein lining of the envelope and see the internal arrangement of ribonucleoprotein complexes.

Electron tomography is a three-dimensional imaging technique that is similar to the clinical imaging technique called computerized axial tomography (CAT scan). The major difference is that electron tomography is done inside an electron microscope and is on a microminiaturized scale. This work has made it possible to pick out the unique features of highly virulent strains of the virus. It has also helped to provide new ideas and insights as to how the virus can determine the most vulnerable cells and infect them. This work should also allow us to determine how antibodies are able to inactivate the virus.[1]

NAMING VIRAL STRAINS

Type A subtypes are identified and named using a very specific system. The geographic location where the strain was first isolated is followed by a laboratory identification number that usually tells how many cases were identified and isolated. Then comes the year of discovery and finally, in parentheses, the type of HA and NA the viral strain possesses. A typical example might be A/Hong Kong/156/97/(H5N1). Another example is A/Singapore/6/86/(H1N1). Scientists need to know this information so they can prepare an appropriate vaccine against the particular influenza virus strain causing the most recent outbreak.

CHANGES IN THE VIRAL GENOME

The influenza virus is constantly changing through **mutations, reassortments**, and recombinations. Different subtypes of influenza A are found in the environment each winter.

In November 2004 the National Institute of Allergy and Infectious Disease (NIAID) announced that it would join forces with a number of scientific partners to begin

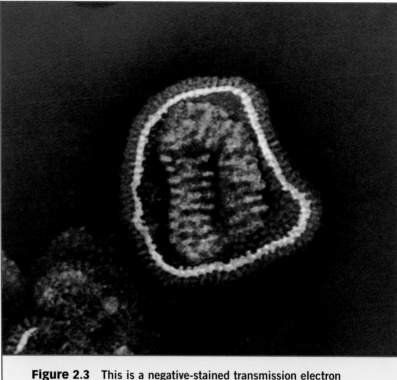

Figure 2.3 This is a negative-stained transmission electron micrograph of a flu virus. (CDC/Dr. Erskine L. Palmer; Dr. M. L. Martin)

an influenza genome-sequencing project. NIAID is a part of the National Institutes of Health (NIH). The group included the National Center for Biotechnology Information of the NIH National Library of Medicine; the Centers for Disease Control and Prevention (CDC); St. Jude Children's Research Hospital; the Wadsworth Center of the New York State Department of Health in Albany, New York; the Armed Forces Institute of Pathology in Washington, D.C.; and the Institute for Genomics Research (TIGR). The objective of the project was to learn how influenza viruses evolve, how the viruses are transmitted, and how they cause disease. It was suggested that this project is the influenza equivalent of the Human Genome Project.[2]

In October 2005 scientists at TIGR announced they had captured influenza evolution in action. The scientists had sequenced 209 complete genomes of the human influenza A virus. Samples came from county clinic patients in New York State over a five-year period (1999–2004). The study showed that there were at least three distinct subpopulations, or variants, of the influenza A virus in circulation during the five-year study period. Some of these variants were circulating through the population at the same time, which meant that some New York residents were contracting different variations of the influenza A virus. This information helped to explain why the 2003–2004 vaccine was not as protective as it should have been. New variants arise from reassortment of genetic materials. The variant mixes with the current dominant strand, resulting in a new viral strain. Steven Salzberg, the senior author of the *Nature* paper detailing the study, indicates that these influenza subpopulations represent a pool of genetic resources that can be drawn upon by the virus. As pockets of these distinct strains spread locally, the influenza virus continues to evolve in a number of directions.[3]

By February 2008 more than 2,900 human and avian genomes from worldwide samples had been sequenced. NIAID director Dr. Anthony Fauci said that "scientists from around the world can use the sequence data to compare different strains of the virus, identify the genetic factors that determine their virulence, and look for new therapeutic, vaccine, and diagnostic targets." All of the sequence data is freely available to the scientific community and the public through the Internet-accessible database called GenBank. The original sequencing group has been expanded to include a number of international laboratories and hospitals. [4]

Therefore, a new flu vaccine must be produced each year. There are two conditions that are frequently mentioned as the major reasons for the instability of the influenza virus. First, small changes in the genetic sequence of the HA or NA genes lead to a change in the amino acid sequence of the HA or NA proteins. This happens because the order, or sequence, of amino acids that make up a protein determine what type of protein will be produced. These changes often occur because the influenza virus is an RNA virus. RNA viruses, with few exceptions, are constantly making "spelling errors" in their genetic sequences when they are being copied. The RNA copying process is flawed. This leads to new genetic sequences. New genetic sequences, in turn, lead to new amino acids being put into place in the creation of a protein. This usually leads to a new or altered protein. This series of continual changes is known as **genetic drift**. The HA protein plays a large role in stimulating immunity (protection against infectious disease); thus changes in this protein may cause a loss of immunity to the virus. NA protein plays a very minor role in immunity.

A second process, known as **genetic shift**, occurs when there is a large, sudden change in the HA or NA proteins, and over time they create major changes in the proteins. This may lead to production of new HA or NA proteins unlike any previously known and to new viral strains against which the population has no immunity. When two strains of virus infect a cell at the same time, the genetic information may not only be copied incorrectly but may also be reassorted or recombined in new ways. This also could lead to strains of viruses that could cause major epidemics or pandemics because the population has no protection against these new strains.

WHY FLU THRIVES IN COLD WEATHER

The annual outbreak of the flu has always been associated with colder weather. Colds seem to occur throughout the year, but the flu and winter are always linked. In the northern hemisphere the flu season is November to March. In the southern hemisphere it is from May to September, and the tropical regions have no obvious flu season. Two recent studies have begun to unravel the reasons for this linkage.

Dr. Peter Palese is professor and chair of the microbiology department of Mount Sinai School of Medicine in New York. He and his research group began to develop ideas using a study published about the 1918 flu pandemic. A 1919 study had indicated that laboratory guinea pigs began to die soon after the influenza epidemic had reached Camp Cody in New Mexico, the site of the study. In a 2006 study Dr. Palese exposed a series of guinea pigs to the flu virus and found that they did indeed get the flu and spread it among the other lab guinea pigs. Dr. Palese's group varied the air temperature and humidity in the guinea pig chambers and found that transmission peaked at 41 degrees Fahrenheit. Transmission of the flu virus decreased as the temperature rose, and it ceased at 86 degrees Fahrenheit. The same results were seen as the humidity increased from 20 percent (highest rate of transmission) to 80 percent (transmission ceasing). While the cooler temperatures were clearly indicative of greater stability of the virus, it was not clear why the cooler temperatures allowed infected animals to continue to release the virus for an extended time period. [5]

The answer to the question of why colder temperatures were conducive to influenza transmission was suggested in an article by Joshua Zimmerberg and his colleagues. Zimmerberg works at the Laboratory of Cellular and Molecular Biophysics in the National Institute of Child Health and Human Development (NICHD). The NICHD is one of the National Institutes of Health. Zimmerberg's group examined the structure of the outer covering of the influenza virus. To view this outer covering they used a form of nuclear magnetic resonance imaging (MRI). This outer covering of the flu and other respiratory viruses is constructed from a "fatty protein" known as hemagglutinin. This is the same protein from which flu vaccines are made, and it represents the "H" in the flu virus name.

The group found that when the virus entered the warm environs of the mouth, the outer covering began to liquefy, enabling the virus to infect the cells lining the respiratory tract. It seems that the virus is capable of infecting the cells only when the viral coat is in the liquid state. The colder weather allows the outer cover to harden, providing a means of insulation for the virus. Zimmerberg found that the covering does not harden all at once. He observed that the covering solidified slowly from 104 degrees down to 39 degrees Fahrenheit. In the warmer outdoor temperatures found during the summer months the covering melts and the virus is destroyed, often by ultraviolet solar radiation. There is some additional concern that this harder covering of the virus in wintertime may make it more difficult to wash the viruses off the hands and other surfaces and may make the virus more resistant to soap and detergents. The good news is that this study provides some new ideas for research in dealing with flu outbreaks. [6]

DETERMINATION OF NEW VACCINE COMPONENTS

The World Health Organization (WHO) makes the decision as to which strains of the virus to include in the new vaccine. Each year they analyze information that is provided by WHO laboratories in Atlanta, Georgia; London, England; Melbourne, Austalia; and Tokyo, Japan. These laboratories observe the dominant strains that were circulating the previous winter. They also look for evidence of new strains with the potential to spread, particularly if the current vaccines do not provide protection against these new strains. A new vaccine usually contains three components: two subtypes of influenza type A and one of influenza type B.

In February 2002, the WHO announced that a new strain of influenza virus had been isolated. The strain, called subtype A/(H1N2), appears to be a combination of two human subtypes that have been causing sickness for a number of years. This new strain probably has arisen from the reassortment of genetic information in the subtypes A/(H1N1) and A/(H3N2). This new strain was identified in China in 1988–1989, but there was no spread of the virus at that time. This new subtype A/(H1N2) strain has been isolated from people in England, Wales, Israel, and Egypt. Because this new subtype is a combination of genetic information from A/(H1N1) and A/(H3N2), people who have been previously vaccinated against these two strains should have a high level of immunity. Even those individuals who have not been previously vaccinated should have some immunity because these strains have been around for a number of years.

The composition of the influenza vaccine for the 2002–2003 season was announced by the WHO on February 6, 2002. This vaccine is designed to be used for the winter months in the Northern Hemisphere. The contents of the vaccine will include:

- an A/New Caledonia/20/99 (H1N1)-like virus

- an A/Moscow/10/99 (H3N2)-like virus (the widely used vaccine strain is A/Panama/2007/99)

- a B/Hong Kong/330/2001—a B Victoria-like virus

The first two components are the same as those found in the 2002 vaccine. Scientists felt that they would provide good protection against this new strain. Recommendations for the vaccine that needed to be produced for the Southern Hemisphere was made by WHO in September 2002. This is the vaccine that was used in May 2003 through October 2003 in the Southern Hemisphere.

In a February 10, 2008, Associated Press news release, Dr. Joseph Breese of the CDC indicated that the influenza vaccine prepared for the 2007–2008 season was not as effective as had been hoped. By some estimates it was only about 40 percent effective. Officials did not include a particular H3N2 strain of influenza A in the vaccine mix for the year. The strain was identified in Brisbane, Australia, in February 2007.

Unfortunately, it was found after the strains for the year's vaccine had been chosen. The World Health Organization felt it was too late to substitute "Brisbane/10" for the current H3N2 strain. There was also concern that they would be unable to find samples of the virus that would grow properly and rapidly enough in the manufacturing process. Unfortunately, that strain turned out to be the dominant strain and was responsible for about 35 percent of the flu cases.

For 2008–2009 the FDA's Vaccines and Related Biological Products Committee (VRBPAC) agreed with the recommendations of the WHO to use the following strains in the vaccine.

- an A/Brisbane/59/2007 (H1N1)-like virus;

- an A/Brisbane/10/2007 (H3N2)-like virus;*

- a B/Florida/4/2006-like virus. **

---

* A/Brisbane/10/2007 is a current Southern Hemisphere vaccine virus.

** B/Florida/4/2006 and B/Brisbane/3/2007 (a B/Florida/4/2006-like virus) are current southern hemisphere vaccine viruses.

These three strains are different from the three used in 2007–2008. Since two of the strains were also recommended for vaccine makers in the Southern Hemisphere in September of 2007, it is hoped that manufacturing and production would not be negatively affected in the Northern Hemisphere.[7]

How do viruses produce copies of themselves in our cells? Should you get vaccinated? Should everyone get vaccinated? Are there any dangers in getting vaccinated?

3

Viral Replication

A virus is an enclosed particle of nucleic acid. It depends on a living cell to carry out the functions we identify with life. It **replicates** only after taking over a living cell. Recall that a virus can be defined as an *intracellular parasite*. A viral genome contains either DNA or RNA but never both. All viruses follow a fairly standardized sequence of actions that allows them to enter host cells.

STEPS IN VIRAL REPLICATION

There are a number of similarities between the way viruses infect bacteria, plants, and animals. The sequence of steps involves: (1) attachment or **adsorption**; (2) penetration; (3) uncoating (most bacterial viruses inject only their nucleic acid and not the entire virus); (4) synthesis of viral enzymes, nucleic acids, and proteins; (5) assembly and packaging; and finally, (6) release of newly formed viruses from the cell. Here concentration focuses on how viruses infect animal cells.

The first part of this process requires that the virus come into contact with the surface of the host cell, find a way to stick to that surface, and introduce the viral genome into the cell (Figure 3.1). This first step is usually called attachment or adsorption. Adsorption means to adhere or stick to a surface. To be successful, the virus must come into contact with a proper receptor protein embedded in the host cell's membrane. A proper receptor is one whose shape is complementary to some part of the viral outer covering. Not all viruses can infect all types of cells because the proper receptors are found only on certain cells. Genetic information on how to make these protein receptor sites is inherited; thus a person with missing or defective information may be less susceptible to certain viral disorders.

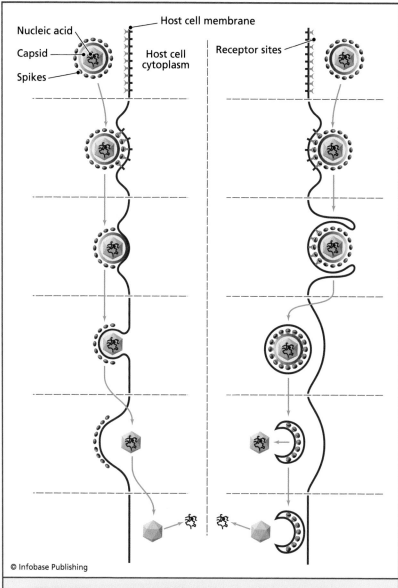

Nucleic acid

Capsid

Spikes

Host cell membrane

Host cell
cytoplasm

Receptor sites

© Infobase Publishing

Figure 3.1   A virus can enter a cell in one of two ways. On the
left, receptor sites on the cell wall attach to the virus and the virus
is sucked onto the cell. The other method of entry is receptor-
mediated endocytosis, shown on the right side. The host cell forms
"arms" that pulls the virus into the cell.

This is true regarding the attachment site for the human immunodeficiency virus (**HIV**). Persons lacking or having imperfect receptor sites on their white blood cells will not convert from being HIV-positive (also known as antibody-positive or virus-positive) to having acquired immunodeficiency syndrome (**AIDS**). The HIV cannot enter the white blood cell or other types of cells such as nerve cells that lack the proper receptors. Drugs that can block or prevent entrance of the virus into the receptor sites are currently under investigation for several viral diseases.

The second step is usually called penetration. In the case of infection of animal cells, the entire virus is taken inside the cell. The viral envelope may fuse with the host cell membrane, thereby causing the lipids in the membrane of the host cell to rearrange. This rearrangement allows the nucleocapsid to enter the cytoplasm of the host cell. A different penetration method occurs when the host cell creates a little pocket, or invagination, in the membrane and surrounds and encloses the attached virus. This method of enclosure is called **receptor-mediated endocytosis**, and the virus is enclosed in a structure sometimes known as a coated vesicle or an endosome. Figure 3.1 shows both methods. Finally, the viral nucleic acid is separated from the protein capsid, a process known as uncoating. In some viruses, digestive enzymes released by the lysosomes of the host cell aid the uncoating. Lysosomes are organelles found in eukaryotic cells. The lysosomes contain a variety of hydrolytic or digestive enzymes. Depending on viral type, the processes of attachment, penetration, and uncoating may take from minutes to as long as 36 hours.

At this point, differences occur in the way the DNA-containing viruses and the RNA-containing viruses continue the process. Figure 3.2 shows how DNA-containing viruses proceed. DNA viruses contain all the genetic information necessary to produce the enzymes that direct the synthesis of the viral components. The virus will use molecules provided by the host cell to

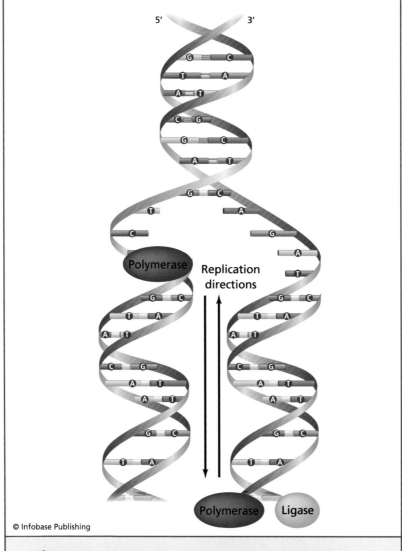

© Infobase Publishing

Figure 3.2   After the virus has successfully entered the host, it begins to replicate. Using the host cell's machinery, the viral DNA unwinds and each strand is copied. This process is aided by two enzymes, polymerase and ligase. Each new set of viral DNA is packaged into a capsule and released from the host cell. These new viruses can now infect other cells and continue the replication process.

construct more viruses. Some DNA viruses carry out this process completely in the host cell's cytoplasm. Other DNA viruses, like the adenoviruses that cause the common cold, divide the work. Viral DNA is copied in the nucleus of the host cell, while the viral proteins are produced in the cytoplasm. As the viral genome is being copied, synthesis of materials that would be used by the host cell is halted. The proteins that will form the capsid of the virus enter the nucleus and combine with the newly copied DNA of the viral genome. A new viral particle or **virion** is formed. The formation of new virions is called assembly or maturation. The new virions then force their way through the membranes. The membrane is pushed in front of them and, as the virus is released from the cell, some of the membrane is removed and forms the new envelope of the virus. This process of forcing the virion through the membrane is called budding and usually kills the host cell.

RNA-containing viruses have a variety of different patterns of synthesis. Some RNA viruses are single-stranded (ssRNA) and some are double-stranded (dsRNA). In some ssRNA viruses, the RNA strand is used directly as a messenger RNA (mRNA) molecule that conveys information on how to make proteins. Such a virus is said to have "sense" or is called a sense or (+) positive-stranded RNA virus. The viruses that cause polio, hepatitis A, and the common cold all are (+) stranded RNA viruses. These viruses are able to supply the genetic information as soon as they have penetrated and uncoated. Some of the newly formed viral proteins inhibit the synthesis activities of the host cell.

Other ssRNA viruses synthesize a complementary strand of RNA. The newly created strand is used as a messenger RNA to guide protein synthesis. Multiple copies of this new (+) strand are usually made. The rules followed in virology suggest that the strand that serves as the mRNA is always said to be (+). The enzyme, RNA polymerase, also known as replicase, is used to synthesize this complementary strand. The host cells do not produce the RNA polymerase used by these viruses. The virus must bring in this version of the enzyme when it penetrates the host cell. The original viral strand is said to have "antisense," and the virus is said to be an antisense virus or (-) stranded RNA virus. The rabies, Ebola, and influenza viruses are (-) stranded RNA viruses.

The group of single-stranded RNA viruses known as retroviruses includes agents that cause various kinds of cancer and AIDS. These viruses convert their RNA into DNA but go through an intermediate DNA stage. The ssRNA is converted into ssDNA, which is then converted into dsDNA; this can now produce mRNA. The unique enzyme required to convert RNA into DNA is known as reverse transcriptase. The process of converting DNA into mRNA is normally called **transcription** and, as can be seen, viruses go through several additional steps to bring this about. The host cell does not produce the enzyme called reverse transcriptase; thus, the retroviruses carry the reverse transcriptase enzyme in their virion (the complete viral particle).

REPLICATION OF THE INFLUENZA VIRUS

The influenza virus is a (-) stranded, enveloped RNA virus that will multiply only in a vertebrate host. It is a member of the family Orthomyxoviridae and the orthomyxovirus group (any virus belonging to that family). Recall that there are three major types of the influenza virus—A, B, and C. The influenza virus invades the cells lining the respiratory tract. The specificity of this relationship is the result of the receptor molecules on the attachment sites of the host cells that closely match the protein molecules extending from the surface of the virus. Also recall that eight linear sections of RNA, containing 10 genes, comprise the viral genome of influenza viruses A and B. Type C has only seven RNA segments. Thus, the influenza genome is said to be a segmented genome. An envelope consisting of several virus-specific protein spikes and lipids derived from host cells covers the nucleocapsid of the influenza virus.

The viral glycoprotein spikes known as hemagglutinin (HA) accomplish the initial attachment of the influenza virus to receptive cells in the respiratory tract. These HAs attach to a molecule of sugar called sialic acid. Sialic acid is derived from neuraminic acid and is a part of the glycoproteins embedded in the host cell membrane. Immunity to influenza occurs when these HA molecules are prevented from attaching to sialic acid by antibodies.

Attachment induces the host cell to engulf the virus through receptor-mediated endocytosis. The membrane of the vesicle or endosome, which has enclosed the virus, fuses with the viral outer surface and allows the virion to enter the host cell. Critical experiments in the 1980s showed that this fusion could not occur unless the pH in the endosome was low, about 5.0. The low pH causes the HA proteins to unfold and change their shape. This allows the lipoprotein envelope of the virus to fuse with the lipid-bilayer membrane of the endosome. As part of this process, the RNA of the virion is released into the cytoplasm of the host cell and migrates to the nucleus. A protein in the membrane of the endosome forms a channel that allows protons (hydrogen ions) to enter the virion. These protons aid in the release of proteins binding the nucleocapsid and allow the nucleocapsid to be moved to the nucleus of the host cell. Internal proteins, including RNA polymerase, soon follow the migration route. Within the host cell nucleus, (-) stranded RNA makes a complementary copy of its genome, which becomes mRNA. This mRNA can be used to make more proteins and more copies of the viral genome. Figure 3.3 shows an overview of the process.

The influenza virus uses the host cell DNA to produce mRNA and then removes part of this newly formed mRNA to attach to its own viral mRNA. These added sequences, sometimes known as caps, allow the viral mRNA to move into the cytoplasm and use the host's ribosomes to produce more viral proteins. The influenza type A virus uses the internal machinery of the nucleus in another way as well.

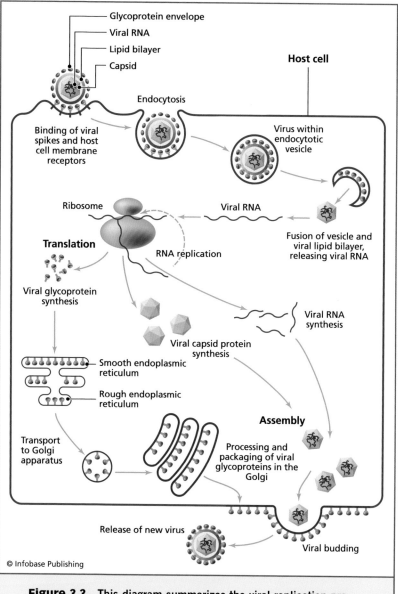

Glycoprotein envelope
Viral RNA
Lipid bilayer
Capsid

Host cell

Endocytosis

Binding of viral
spikes and host
cell membrane
receptors

Virus within
endocytotic
vesicle

Ribosome

Viral RNA

Translation

RNA replication

Fusion of vesicle and
viral lipid bilayer,
releasing viral RNA

Viral glycoprotein
synthesis

Viral RNA
synthesis

Viral capsid protein
synthesis

Smooth endoplasmic
reticulum

Rough endoplasmic
reticulum

Assembly

Transport
to Golgi
apparatus

Processing and
packaging of viral
glycoproteins in the
Golgi

Release of new virus

Viral budding

© Infobase Publishing

Figure 3.3   This diagram summarizes the viral replication process. First, the virus must enter the host cell. Next, the virus will shed its protein coat and begin replication. While genetic material is replicating, the virus will also produce a new glycoprotein coat. Finally, the new copies of the virus are assembled and released from the cell.

Two of the eight RNA segments in the virus contain genetic information, which produces mRNA molecules that can be spliced together. The host cell nucleus has the machinery to do this splicing. When mRNA molecules are spliced together,

SPREADING THE WEALTH

The cells most frequently attacked by the influenza viruses are cells in the lungs and throat. The reason is simple. These cells contain receptors that allow the hemagglutinin (HA) a site for attachment. HA is one of the two major proteins that are part of the viral envelope. To form this attachment, the HA needs to be cut into two pieces. This is accomplished by enzymes called proteases, common in the lungs and throat but not in other parts of the body. This is why influenza is usually just a respiratory disease. If the HA is not split by the proteases, the virus cannot infect the host cell.

In 2005, researchers at the University of Wisconsin, led by Dr. Yoshihiro Kawaoka, discovered that the most deadly forms of influenza type A use an additional enzyme to infect cells throughout the body, not just in the lungs and throat. The additional enzyme is called plasmin and is found in all sorts of tissue. The second major protein making up the envelope is an enzyme protein known as neuraminidase (NA). The NA of these deadly flu strains collects and attaches a molecule called plasminogen. Plasminogen is converted into plasmin. Thus, the virus is providing itself with a high concentration of a molecule that will allow it to infect cells throughout the body.

Kawaoka and his group tested 10 other strains of flu and could not find the same enzyme being used. Only the form that was a descendant of the 1918 pandemic strain used the enzyme plasmin. The researchers hope that this information may provide a means of testing individuals to see if they are harboring the most dangerous forms of influenza. Perhaps a new target for drug therapy may also come from this information.

a new message is created, allowing the cell to make a different protein. The end result of this splicing process is that the eight RNA segments can produce up to ten viral mRNAs. Assembly of the new viruses occurs when the capsid proteins surround the newly formed viral RNA molecules. Together with other proteins, the new virions move toward the host cell membrane.

An international team of researchers used a novel approach to find the answer to the question of how the influenza virus organizes its genetic information. The team used electron tomography to produce a virtual dissection of the virus. Creating a series of serial sections led to a consistent cross-sectional view of the virus. The team found that the influenza virus has a very specific way in which it packages its genetic information. This work also clarified the question of whether viruses assembled their genetic information in a systematic way or in a random way. The viruses systematically arranged the RNA fragments in a circle of seven fragments in touch with the viral membrane and with another fragment in the center. This understanding makes it possible to begin developing new antiviral drugs. It also opens the door into using benign influenza viruses as carriers or vectors for vaccine production. By changing the arrangement of the genetic materials scientists may be able to get the virus to mass produce vaccines. This same strategy might be useful in developing vaccines for other viral diseases such as HIV/AIDS.

Some of the proteins that the virus has instructed the host cell to make become glycoproteins for the envelope of the new virions. These proteins follow the standard route of construction on the ribosomes, which are attached to a series of membrane channels known as the endoplasmic reticulum (ER) of the host cell. This rough ER, as it is known, produces a protein channel to the interior of the ER when construction of the protein has been completed on the ribosome. A research team led by Thomas Rapoport of Harvard University discovered

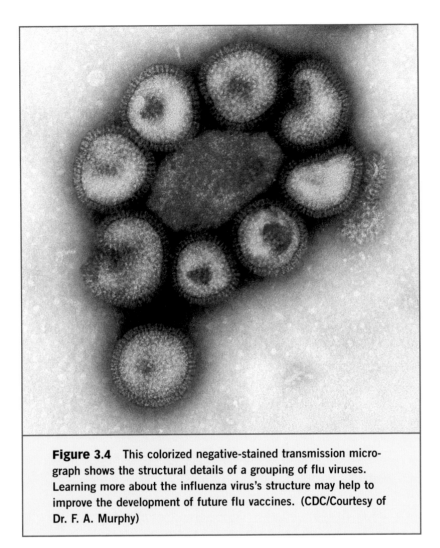

Figure 3.4 This colorized negative-stained transmission micro-graph shows the structural details of a grouping of flu viruses. Learning more about the influenza virus's structure may help to improve the development of future flu vaccines. (CDC/Courtesy of Dr. F. A. Murphy)

these protein translocation channels. The results were reported in the journal *Cell* on November 5, 1996. As the newly formed protein enters the ER, a portion of the protein is enzymatically removed. This removal causes the channel to close. The portion of the protein that is removed had been serving as a signal to the ER membrane. The protein is packaged by lipids in the ER and sent to the organelle known as Golgi. Within the Golgi apparatus the appropriate sugars are added, thus forming the new glycoproteins, which are transported to the host cell membrane and become embedded within it. The glycoproteins, along with the viral proteins, hemagglutinin, and neuraminidase, become part of a new viral envelope.

The newly formed virions are now ready to leave the host cell. This process, known as budding, may take as long as 6 hours. The cell is not killed immediately but eventually dies owing to the disruption of its normal synthesis of various essential molecules. The nucleocapsids of the new viruses bind to the inner surface of the host cell membrane. Remember that the virus originally attached to the host membrane by binding to sialic acid (neuraminic acid). The host membrane is studded with these molecules, and the newly formed virions now have them attached to their surfaces. If these sialic acid molecules are not removed from the host cell membrane and the outside of the virions, the virions will stick to each other and to the host cell membrane. The protein neuraminidase (NA) is an enzyme that breaks down sialic acid (neuramininic acid) in both the host cell membrane and on the surface of the new virions. Removal of the sialic acid molecule allows the virus to leave the host cell in which it was formed.

As shown in Figure 3.5, this budding process takes some of the cell membrane and the embedded proteins to form the new viral envelope. Nine different forms of neuraminidase have been identified for influenza A virus. About one-third of the amino acid sequence of the neuraminidase molecule is the same in all nine forms. This amino acid sequence provides the structure of the portion of the enzyme that binds to the sialic acid molecule. Neuraminidase-inhibitor drugs, such as Tamiflu (ogeltamivir), block that site of attachment, meaning viruses cannot leave the cell to invade other cells and would stick to each other.

Some have suggested that viruses are simple structures. Perhaps, but they need to look more carefully at how complex

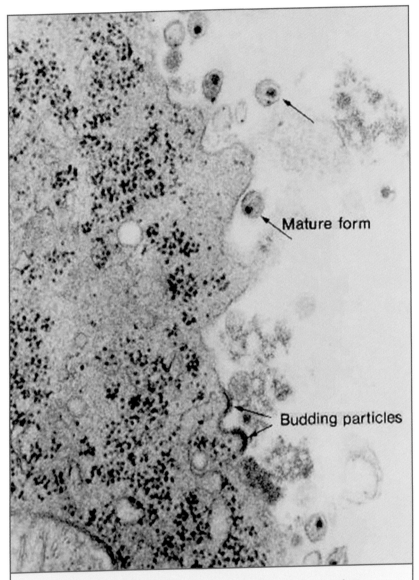

Figure 3.5 This electron micrograph of the HIV-1 virus shows the budding stage of replication. Budding is the way in which newly created viruses are released from the host cells. These new viruses contain all the genetic material of the original virus and can infect new cells and continue to replicate. (Courtesy CDC/ Alyne Harrison, Erskine Palmer, Paul Feorino)

these so-called simple structures really are. In the next three chapters, this text will follow a college freshman as he comes into contact with some unwanted invaders, the influenza viruses. These chapters will focus on treatment possibilities, diagnostic tests available, and ways to prevent the influenza virus from making one sick. Subsequent chapters will explore the possible complications that can arise when one becomes infected and ways that the body tries to protect and defend itself.

4

"I've Got the Flu. What Can I do?"

Friday night's concert was great. Even though it was November and cold outside, thousands had jammed together to hear "Dice and the Slicers," the latest singing rage. Jim and his friends left the Civic Center hoarse from yelling. They stopped at their usual hangout, Paul's Pizza Palace and rejoined some of their friends. The ice-cold soda and piping-hot sausage and mushroom pizza tasted wonderful. On Saturday Jim finally got up at 1 P.M. The rest of Saturday was a blur. Sunday evening was devoted to finishing up some homework and studying for his Principles of Biology class. There was a big lab exam coming up on Thursday.

On Monday, the alarm went off at 6 A.M. It sounded like a giant gong banging inside Jim's head. Turning on the light nearly blinded him and added to the pain of his pounding head. Jim's throat was dry and had a tickling sensation. When he coughed, it was a dry, sometimes raspy, cough. Jim started to shiver and realized that most of his muscles ached. He felt hot and was exhausted. "What's going on?" groaned Jim. "What did I eat to cause this feeling?" Jim tried to stand up but felt like he had been beaten with a baseball bat. He fell back into bed and immediately regretted that move. His head was pounding like the drummer on Friday night. Only this time, his head was the drum.

BE SURE IT'S REALLY THE FLU
Jim is showing most of the classic symptoms of influenza—the "flu." Did you recognize the symptoms? Headache, fever, chills, dry cough,

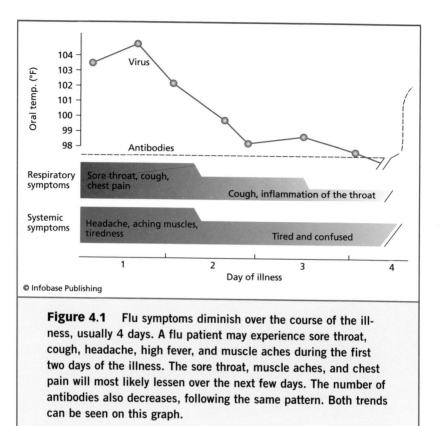

Figure 4.1 Flu symptoms diminish over the course of the illness, usually 4 days. A flu patient may experience sore throat, cough, headache, high fever, and muscle aches during the first two days of the illness. The sore throat, muscle aches, and chest pain will most likely lessen over the next few days. The number of antibodies also decreases, following the same pattern. Both trends can be seen on this graph.

fatigue, and really achy muscles are the starting symptoms. There are many diseases that cause flulike symptoms. Some are bacterial, some are fungal, and some are viral. If a person can get up and go to work or school, it is very unlikely that he or she has the flu. Jim doesn't sound like he is going anywhere very soon. He wondered if he had eaten something to cause these symptoms. People sometimes use the term "stomach flu." This condition is not the flu. It can be caused by one of several viruses. The rotavirus causes stomach flu, which occurs during the same time of the year as the influenza virus. Other enteric (intestinal) viruses and the Norwalk virus all cause stomach flu. Norwalk viruses cause a vomiting disease during the winter, and all stomach flu viruses cause vomiting and/or diarrhea. Another disease sometimes diagnosed as stomach flu is actually gastroenteritis, which is usually caused by bacteria. Stomach flu is sometimes misdiagnosed as viral gastroenteritis as well.

Could Jim have a cold or a strep throat (throat infection caused by bacteria)? The comparisons in Table 4.1 may help to answer part of that question.

Cold symptoms normally include stuffy, runny nose, sneezing, sore throat, and cough. Symptoms of a cold usually do not include a fever or body aches. Jim does not have these symptoms. Strep throat symptoms include a high fever, difficulty swallowing, headache, fatigue, and coughing. Strep throat is caused by a bacterium of the genus *Streptococcus*. Jim certainly has those symptoms. Strep throat patients also have swollen lymph glands and a red, raw appearance to the back of the throat. If Jim could get to the doctor, he could find out which disease he has. There are a number of rapid tests that can be done in the doctor's office for identification of strep infections. Since there are a high number of cases of flu in the community at the present time, Jim's doctor will probably suggest that Jim does in fact have the flu. A quick call to some of his friends from the concert showed that three of them had the same symptoms as Jim. Their doctors also diagnosed their illnesses as the flu.

I'VE GOT THE FLU

It seems that almost all doctors agree what you should do when you have the flu. First, be sure to get plenty of bed rest. Do not try to be a hero and drag yourself to work or school. If you come into contact with other people, you are a menace in a number of ways: going to work or school, while you are there, and on your way home. You could become sleepy while driving or while at work or school. Worse, you also could be spreading influenza to your work or schoolmates. Second, drink plenty of fluids. Try to drink water and not alcoholic or caffeinated drinks. Third, take over-the-counter medications to relieve the major symptoms. Remember that these medications reduce your discomfort. They do not treat the viral infection itself. Most physicians recommend acetaminophen-based products, such as Tylenol, to relieve the fever and aches. The fever may last from 2 to 5 days. Acetaminophen products are less likely to irritate the stomach. Aspirin and aspirin-based products sometimes irritate the stomach lining. They may also play a role in the development of a rare liver and

Table 4.1 How to Tell If It Is a Cold or a Flu

Symptoms	Cold	Flu
How did the illness occur?	Gradually	Suddenly
Do you have a fever?	Rarely	May be higher than 101°F (38°C) and last 3–4 days
Do you feel exhausted?	Never or only a little	Very and happened suddenly
Is your throat sore?	Usually	Not usually
Are you coughing?	A hacking, sometimes severe cough	A dry, hoarse, or raspy cough
Are you sneezing?	Usually	Sometimes
Do you have aches and pains?	Occasional aches and pains	Frequently achy, sometimes very sore
Do you have a headache?	Not usually	It is strong and nasty
Do you have a runny nose?	Yes	No, usually dry and clear
Do you have chills?	No	Yes
How is your appetite?	Normal	Decreased

central nervous system condition known as Reye's syndrome. This condition shows up most frequently in children under 18 years of age. It may cause vomiting, convulsions, brain damage, and even death. If your flu symptoms include congestion, coughing, and a runny nose, you may also take decongestants and antihistamines. There are a number of over-the-counter flu remedies that contain both of these ingredients. There are a number of excellent references that provide information about caring for a patient at home. The "Home Care Fact Sheet" is one of the best, covering everything from setting up a sick room at home to providing tables to input data about the patient's fluid levels.[1]

TREATMENT REGIMES—PRESCRIPTION DRUGS

It is important that you see your doctor within 48 hours of having noticed your symptoms. There are **antiviral** drugs available that can reduce both the severity and length of the disease, although only by a few days. These drugs must be given within 48 hours of the appearance of symptoms for maximum effectiveness and require a doctor's prescription.

The first of these drugs is amantadine. It goes by the brand name of Symmetrel. The second drug is known as rimantadine, or the brand name Flumadine. Both of these drugs work only on type A influenza virus and will not work on types B or C. Flumadine is less toxic. Individuals with cases of uncomplicated type A influenza may be given amantadine for 5 days. The usual dose is 200 mg. Rimantadine is usually given in 100 mg doses twice a day for 5 days. Recently, type A viral subtypes resistant to both of these drugs have been found, and rimantadine and amantadine are no longer recommended for routine care.

Two other drugs have been developed that can be used to treat both types A and B influenza. These drugs, zanamivir (Relenza) and oseltamivir (Tamiflu), are part of a group of drugs that attack a different site on the virus. Relenza and

Tamiflu attack and inhibit the enzyme neuraminidase (NA), which is a prominent part of the viral coat. Relenza is available in nasal spray form only, whereas Tamiflu can be taken orally. Both have been shown to have very few clinical side effects. Relenza can be used as a treatment for those who are 12 years of age and older. Tamiflu is used as a treatment for those who are 18 years of age and older. Tamiflu can be given preventively to individuals who are 13 years of age or older to prevent them from coming down with flu. Relenza is not used as a preventative. Tamiflu is currently the most widely prescribed antiviral medication for influenza. Unfortunately, it is also more expensive than Symmetrel and Flumadine. Unfortunately, there is now increasing resistance to these drugs in influenza strains. It is not a good idea to call your doctor to ask for an antibiotic unless you know you are dealing with a bacterial infection. **Antibiotics** do not work against viruses.

YOU AND YOUR DOCTOR

It is important to see the doctor when symptoms first appear. Only in this way can a strep or another infection be ruled out. If it is a strep infection, appropriate antibiotics can be prescribed. If it is the flu, the doctor may prescribe one of the previously mentioned antiviral medications. Sometimes infection with the influenza virus can be complicated by other viruses, bacteria, or fungi. If the patient becomes breathless or begins to slip in and out of consciousness, call the doctor. If he or she becomes confused or delirious, call the doctor. As is true with most diseases, the patient has a better chance of recovering completely and rapidly if he or she takes positive action to treat the disease and its symptoms.

Could Jim have prevented getting the flu? What could he have done? What should he do in the future? There is no question that the principal way to prevent getting the flu is to get vaccinated. However, in recent years people have become more aware that various viruses, including the cold and influenza viruses, are transmitted on people's hands which, in turn, contact just about everything. This has led to the growth of hand sanitizers in recent years.

In 2005 and 2007, The Alliance for Consumer Education (ACE) administered a nationwide germ study to determine the overall awareness of mothers as to how cold and flu germs are

INFLUENZA AND RELATED DISEASES

On May 11, 1997, a three-year-old boy in Hong Kong was having difficulty breathing. He was hospitalized on May 15 and diagnosed as having pneumonia and Reye's syndrome.

One of the problems associated with influenza is the damage that it does to lung tissue. The tissue becomes swollen and inflamed. This damage is usually slight and heals within a few weeks. However, the immune system of a young child often responds slowly to the rapid growth of the virus.

Pneumonia is an inflammation of the lungs caused by different viruses or bacteria. Reye's syndrome affects the brain and liver of a child who is recovering from a viral infection like influenza. Nausea and vomiting are followed by confusion and delirium. As the liver breaks down, the chemistry of the blood begins to change. Most victims of Reye's syndrome sustain some degree of brain damage. This syndrome is associated with taking aspirin-based products. Therefore, aspirin should NEVER be given to children under 12 years of age who are suffering from flulike symptoms.

On May 21, 1997, the young boy died. It was reported that he had died from complications of the flu. He was the first victim in the 1997 group of individuals who died from a strain of influenza found in chickens. This was the first time that this strain showed up in humans. By November of 1997, more cases appeared, and the world was made aware of a new type of flu.

spread. The second part of the study asked mothers to indicate the most effective ways to prevent and/or contain colds and flu. The 2007 study showed that there had been a greater than 10 percent increase in mothers who felt that keeping their house clean was the most effective way to protect against colds and flu. There had been an equally large increase in the percentage of mothers who said that they clean the surfaces of their children's

In May 2002, several members of the United Kingdom task force serving in Afghanistan fell ill. Their symptoms included fever, headache, and general gastroenteritis. Since medical diagnosis and care are difficult to obtain in a war zone, the individuals were sent to either an American hospital in Germany or back to England. At least three individuals who had been in contact with the original seven members also became ill.

The initial diagnosis suggested that a Norwalk-like virus (NLV) was the cause. NLV seems to cause a common gut infection in England, with as many as one million cases each year. Outbreaks occur in places where people are closely confined and in constant contact with each other, such as schools or hospitals. Military personnel working in close quarters during wartime are also prime candidates. Many cases occurred during the Gulf War (1990–1991).

NLV is seldom dangerous, but unfortunately it is always unpleasant. Diarrhea and explosive fits of vomiting may last from 24 to 48 hours. No specific treatment exists other than making sure that the patient does not become dehydrated. Most people recover within a few days.

The virus is spread when particles from an infected person get into the gut of another person. Poor personal hygiene and particles that become airborne during fits of vomiting are the major means of transfer.

toys on a weekly basis. Parents have made it clear that they understand that the most effective way to reduce exposure to germs is to wash their hands and clean their homes and places of work. Interestingly, more than 60 percent of parents give their children some form of home remedy when the children become ill. The most common home remedy—chicken soup.

5

Diagnosis

How do doctors determine what disease a patient actually has? It has often been suggested that the diagnosis of diseases such as influenza is as much an art as a science. While visible symptoms might suggest the flu, these same symptoms could represent another virus, such as strep throat. Knowing whether the disease is caused by a virus or a bacterium can reduce the problem of taking medicines that might be useless and could cause other unforeseen problems. Bacterial, but not viral, diseases should be treated with the proper antibiotic, but antibiotics are not effective against viruses. One of the biggest challenges faced in medicine today is the number of strains of bacteria that are resistant to one or more antibiotics. The abuse, overuse, and misuse of antibiotics has led to the development of dozens of resistant strains of pathogenic bacteria. If the disease is viral, proper antiviral therapy should be administered when or if available.

When there is an outbreak of some respiratory sickness in the immediate area, it makes sense to test some of the sick patients to determine if influenza is the cause. Many of Jim's friends who had also attended the same concert had been diagnosed with the flu. If many individuals in a local area have similar symptoms, Jim's doctor would likely suggest that he also has the flu. The signs of the illness, known as the clinical symptoms, are often used to make a presumptive diagnosis. Unfortunately, a number of diseases have flulike symptoms, thus reducing the accuracy of a diagnosis based only on the symptoms.

TYPES OF DIAGNOSTIC TESTS AVAILABLE

There are a number of tests that can aid in the diagnosis of influenza. In recent years, rapid diagnostic tests have been developed that can be performed on an outpatient basis. Laboratory results can be given in 30 minutes or less. As might be suspected, these tests differ in terms of which viruses they can detect. Some detect only type A influenza virus, whereas others can detect both type A and type B. Most of these rapid tests have a lower sensitivity than other, longer tests. Thus, a negative result received from one of these rapid tests should still be confirmed with one of the other tests available. None of the rapid tests provide information about influenza A subtypes. Some of these rapid tests are shown below.

In January 2008, the FDA gave its approval for a new test, called the xTAG Respiratory Viral Panel, to be marketed by Luminex Molecular Diagnostics. This test panel is the first of its kind that allows for the identification of various subtypes of influenza A, namely subtypes of H1 and H3. As previously noted in this book, influenza A has been responsible for several major epidemics.

This xTAG Panel is the first that has been approved by the FDA that allows several tests to be processed using the same sample. Called a multiplex platform, this testing procedure is faster at detecting and identifying 12 very specific respiratory

Table 5.1 Viruses Identified by xTAG Respiratory Viral Panel*

Influenza B—one of the 3 types of human influenza, less severe than influenza A, some subtype usually included in flu vaccine mixture
Adenovirus—cause of infections similar to strep throat or tonsillitis
Rhinovirus—most common viral infective agent in humans; major cause of common cold
Parainfluenza 1,2, & 3—all leading factors in common cold and the croup
Respiratory syncytial virus subtypes A & B—leading causes of infant pneumonia and bronchiolitis; contributes to development of long-term pulmonary disease
* in addition to influenza A, subtypes H1 and H

viruses. These 12 viruses account for more than 85 percent of all respiratory viral infections. Jeremy Bridge-Cook, vice president of Luminex Molecular Diagnostics, suggested that test time will vary, but it can be reduced to less than a week, perhaps to as little as 6 hours.

HOW DOES IT WORK?

- A doctor takes a sample from the patient's respiratory tract, usually with a nasopharyngeal swab. The sample is taken to the lab.

- Nucleic acids (DNA and RNA) are removed from the cells in the sample.

- The lab separates and copies the nucleic acids using the polymerase chain reaction, which produces multiple copies of the nucleic acids. The amplified nucleic acids are mixed with chemicals known as primers.

- The DNA and RNA are processed and products bound to specific beads. Each different product will be bound to a differently colored bead.

- Beads are sorted and analyzed by the Luminex xMAP instrument, which reads the test result using lasers to identify the color of the bead and associate it with a specific virus.

- These test results provide the doctor with clear results showing if a particular virus is present. This information is used along with clinical presentation and other laboratory findings to help determine whether the patient has a respiratory viral infection caused by a specific virus.

Bridge-Cook indicated that the cost of the test would probably be in the hundreds of dollars as opposed to the current thousands of dollars required to conduct all of the tests separately.

No matter what type of test is being used, the proper collection of materials to be tested is the most important factor in the procedure. Proper collection techniques are necessary to provide an uncontaminated sample for testing. In this way, virologists can determine the strain of virus causing the disease symptoms and develop the most beneficial treatment. They can also determine if new, previously unidentified, strains of the virus are in circulation. This information can

Table 5.2 Influenza Diagnostic Table

Procedure	Influenza Types Detected	Acceptable Specimens	Time for Results	Rapid result available
Viral culture	A and B	NP swab, throat swab, nasal wash, bronchial wash, nasal aspirate, sputum	3-10 days	No
Immunofluorescence DFA Antibody Staining	A and B	NP swab, nasal wash, bronchial wash, nasal aspirate, sputum	2–4 hours	No
RT-PCR	A and B	NP swab, throat swab, nasal wash, bronchial wash, nasal aspirate, sputum	2–4 hours	No
Serology	A and B	paired acute and convalescent serum samples	2 weeks or more	No
Enzyme Immunoassay (EIA)	A and B	NP swab, throat swab, nasal wash, bronchial wash	2 hours	No
Rapid Diagnostic Tests				
Directigen Flu A (Becton-Dickinson)	A	NP wash and aspirate	less than 30 minutes	Yes
Directigen Flu A+B (Becton-Dickinson)	A and B	NP swab, spirate, wash; lower nasal swab; throat swab; bronchio-alveolar lavage	less than 30 minutes	Yes
Directigen EZ Flu A+B (Becton-Dickinson)	A and B	NP swab, aspirate, wash; lower nasal swab; throat swab; bronchioalveolar lavage	less than 30 minutes	Yes

(continues)

then be used to make decisions about the type of future vaccine to develop.

Three major types of samples are collected for testing: throat swabs, nasal swabs or washes, and nasopharyngeal washes. Experimental evidence suggests that nasopharyngeal washes are more effective than throat swabs in producing findings.

A throat culture should be taken before any antiviral medication is given. The patient is asked to open his or her mouth

FLU OIA (Biostar)	A and B	NP swab, throat swab, nasal aspirate, sputum	less than 30 minutes	Yes
FLU OIA A/B (Biostar)	A and B	NP swab, throat swab, nasal aspirate, sputum	less than 30 minutes	Yes
NOW Influenza A (Binax)	A	Nasal wash/aspirate, NP swab	less than 30 minutes	Yes
NOW Influenza B (Binax)	B	Nasal wash/aspirate, NP swab	less than 30 minutes	Yes
NOW Influenza A&B (Binax)	A and B	Nasal wash/aspirate, NP swab	less than 30 minutes	Yes
OSOM® Influenza A&B (Genzyme)	A and B	Nasal swab	less than 30 minutes	Yes
QuickVue Influenza Test (Quidel)	A and B	NP swab, nasal wash, nasal aspirate	less than 30 minutes	Yes
QuickVue Influenza A+B Test (Quidel)	A and B	NP swab, nasal wash, nasal aspirate	less than 30 minutes	Yes
SAS FluAlert (SA Scientific)	A and B	Nasal wash/aspirate	less than 30 minutes	Yes
TRU FLU (Meridian Bioscience)	A and B	Nasal wash/swab, NP aspirate/swab	less than 30 minutes	Yes
XPECT Flu A&B (Remel)	A and B	Nasal wash, NP swab, throat swab	less than 30 minutes	Yes
ZstatFlu (ZymeTx)	A and B	throat swab	less than 30 minutes	Yes
1. NP = nasopharyngeal 2. Source: CDC				

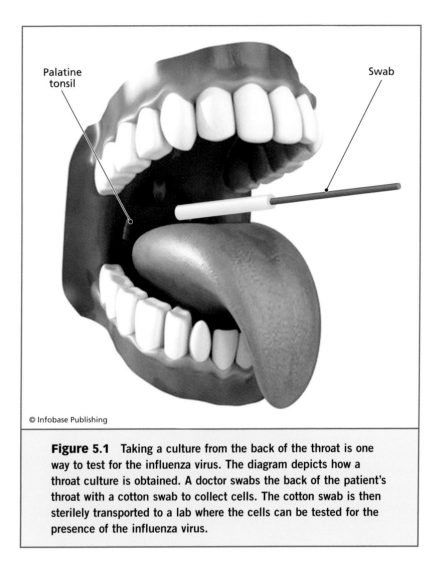

Palatine
tonsil

Swab

© Infobase Publishing

Figure 5.1 Taking a culture from the back of the throat is one way to test for the influenza virus. The diagram depicts how a throat culture is obtained. A doctor swabs the back of the patient's throat with a cotton swab to collect cells. The cotton swab is then sterilely transported to a lab where the cells can be tested for the presence of the influenza virus.

and say "ah." The tongue is gently pressed down with a tongue blade. The patient's throat should be well lit and visible. Using a swab that has been moistened with a solution that will pick up the viruses, the physician gently rubs the swab over the back of the patient's throat. He or she tries to avoid touching the patient's tongue, cheek, or lips with the swab. After the

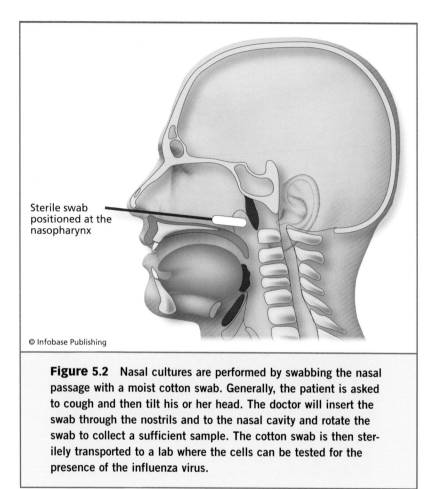

Sterile swab
positioned at the
nasopharynx

© Infobase Publishing

Figure 5.2 Nasal cultures are performed by swabbing the nasal passage with a moist cotton swab. Generally, the patient is asked to cough and then tilt his or her head. The doctor will insert the swab through the nostrils and to the nasal cavity and rotate the swab to collect a sufficient sample. The cotton swab is then sterilely transported to a lab where the cells can be tested for the presence of the influenza virus.

material is collected, the swab is placed in a sterile container and sent to the laboratory.

A nasal swab involves a slightly moistened cotton, Dacron, or polyester swab such as a Q-tips swab. It is used to get a sample of nasal mucus that may contain bacteria or viruses. The swab is inserted about 1 cm (~½ inch) into the nasal cavity and gently rotated. After removal, the sample is placed in a sterile container for transport to the laboratory. Nasal swabs are not as reliable as nasoharyngeal swabs.

For a nasopharyngeal culture, the sterile swab is inserted through the nostril and into the nasopharynx and swirled around. Note from the figure that this is the area over the roof of the mouth. A nasopharyngeal wash requires first that the patient's head be tilted backward at about a 70° angle. A syringe filled with sterile saline has a small piece of tubing attached to its tip. The tubing is used to allow the saline to enter the nostril. The nasal secretions should be removed immediately by a suction device or the patient may tilt his or her head forward and drain the specimen into a sterile container.

VIRAL ISOLATION

Any test used to isolate and grow viral cultures relies on specimen samples taken by any of the previously indicated methods. There are some suggestions in the literature that nasal washings provide the best specimens. Specimen samples may be inoculated into the amniotic cavity of 10- to 12-day-old embryonated chicken eggs or tissue cultures. Using fertilized chicken eggs as a medium for viral cultivation was first proposed by Alice M. Woodruff and Ernest W. Goodpasture in 1931. Viral particles will replicate inside the cells of the amniotic membrane, releasing large numbers of viruses into the amniotic fluid. Various sites within the chicken egg may be inoculated for the cultivation of different viruses. Incubation usually takes 48 to 72 hours. Viruses in the amniotic fluid can be detected after they are mixed with a sample of red blood cells taken from chickens, guinea pigs, or humans. Rhesus monkey cells provide the most sensitive cells for tissue culture, although chicken and human kidney cells are also used. Influenza viruses isolated by either technique can be identified as to type by various serologic (serum) and molecular tests. Identifying influenza viruses as to subtypes and strains is the job of the World Health Organization reference laboratories. To provide the United States with sufficient flu vaccine may require as many as 100 million chicken eggs. Manufacturers

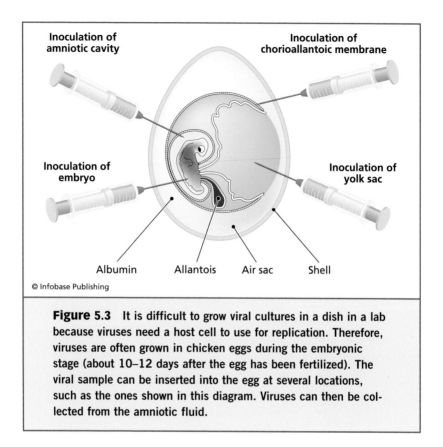

Inoculation of amniotic cavity

Inoculation of chorioallantoic membrane

Inoculation of embryo

Inoculation of yolk sac

Albumin   Allantois   Air sac   Shell

© Infobase Publishing

Figure 5.3   It is difficult to grow viral cultures in a dish in a lab because viruses need a host cell to use for replication. Therefore, viruses are often grown in chicken eggs during the embryonic stage (about 10–12 days after the egg has been fertilized). The viral sample can be inserted into the egg at several locations, such as the ones shown in this diagram. Viruses can then be collected from the amniotic fluid.

of vaccine are looking to alternative sources for growing the viruses needed to produce the vaccine. Cell lines derived from humans, monkeys, and dogs are currently at the top of the list. Using cell culture lines would hasten the production process and reduce the labor involved in the process. It would also make it possible to produce large quantities rapidly in the case of a global pandemic. This is not a new technique since cell cultures are currently used to prepare polio vaccines. The only major problem at this time is the cost of converting production plants to the new cell-based systems. That sound you hear is a collective cluck of relief.

SEROLOGIC TESTS

Often the actual cause of a disease may be difficult to isolate and grow in a culture solution. This is true whether the disease is caused by bacteria or by viruses. It is possible to determine whether one has been in contact with the infectious agent by a simple blood test. **Serology** is the study of the portion of the blood known as the **serum**. Usually, tests using the serum are designed to detect the presence of **antibodies** (Ab) to a specific disease or strain of disease. If the body has been infected with bacteria or viruses in sufficient numbers, the immune system will recognize the foreign particles, cells, or molecules and respond to their presence. Antibodies are specific proteins produced by one type of white blood cell when a foreign invader is recognized. The production of antibodies is a multistep process undertaken by the immune system.

Cells of the immune system, usually modified white blood cells, must first recognize the foreign invader. After these cells recognize and make contact with the foreign invader, a series of chemicals, usually proteins, are released to communicate this information to other parts of the immune system. Finally, action is taken, in this case production of antibodies specific to this foreign invader. This RCA sequence (Recognition, Communication, Action), or some version of it, constitutes the most common immune response. Thus, a strain of influenza will cause infected individuals to produce antibodies specific to that strain. This provides the "footprints" of the foreign invader. Individuals who have antibodies specific to that strain when tested are said to be **seropositive**.

It might be useful to review the structure of blood at this time. Blood consists of a cellular component, sometimes called the formed elements. First are the familiar red blood cells (erythrocytes), responsible for carrying oxygen to our body's cells and carbon dioxide away from the cells. Second are the white blood cells (leukocytes), which are involved in constantly monitoring the body sites for foreign molecules or cells and also involved in the immune response. Some white blood cells are involved in the rejection of foreign tissues or organs. Finally, the platelets (thrombocytes) are involved in the process of blood coagulation or clotting. The remainder of the blood is the liquid portion known as the "plasma." The plasma is about 90 percent water. Dissolved inorganic ions, organic substances, and proteins make up the remainder. Two of the major protein types, fibrinogen and prothrombin, are involved in blood clotting. If we remove the formed elements and the clotting factors, the straw-colored liquid portion that remains is called the serum.

Serologic tests can be used to diagnose influenza using a number of antibody or antigen detection tests. One test, known as the HAI or hemagglutinin-inhibition test, looks for antibodies produced against one type of spike in the viral envelope. One of the rapid tests mentioned earlier, ZstatFlu is designed to detect neuraminidase, the other type of protein enzyme found in the spikes of the envelope. An even more rapid determination can be made by looking for viral antigens. An **antigen** is a molecule, such as a protein, or a cell part, such as a bacterial cell wall, that the host determines is foreign to the body. All of the other rapid test procedures previously mentioned attempt to detect viral antigens.

Viral antigens can be detected in nasal secretions by an immunofluorescence test. In this procedure, fluorescent-tagged molecules will attach only to specific antigens, allowing them to be visualized under a microscope. Although the test can be conducted fairly rapidly, not all laboratories have the capability to carry it out. Some researchers question the specificity of certain parts of this process and often find the interpretation of results difficult because of background changes. There appears to be a great deal of subjectivity in the interpretation of the results.

The polymerase chain reaction (PCR) technique can also be used to detect the presence of antigens. The PCR procedure allows scientists to take a small amount of nucleic acid and make multiple copies of it. In many ways, the PCR machine functions like a copying machine. PCR testing of influenza virus RNA is currently available, but it is of limited use in a typical laboratory setting.

Many clinicians feel that the ELISA (enzyme-linked immunosorbent assay) or EAI test is the best and probably should be the first test used to see if an individual is positive for the suspected viral agent. ELISA or EAI can be used to test for specific antigens or for antigen-specific antibodies. The presence of antigens or antibodies in solution causes the solution to change color. This color change is stimulated by an enzyme. Enzyme immunoassays can be performed rapidly, usually within two hours. There is much less subjectivity in the interpretation of the results, and the test is widely available. The only drawback to the technique is that predictions made from results are not very reliable when the number of antigens or antibodies in the original sample is very low. The Howard Hughes Medical Institute has a virtual laboratory at their online site that enables people to run their own ELISA tests.[1]

All serologic tests have some level of false-positive results caused by a variety of factors. Both the sensitivity and specificity of test results for influenza vary according to the type of sample used, the type of test chosen, and the laboratory personnel who carry out the test. Test results should supplement any other types of clinical information that is available to the physician. Now that it has been seen how influenza can be treated and diagnosed, attention must turn to methods available to prevent its spread.

6

Influenza–Nature's Frequent Flyer: Prevention

Remember Jim? He recovered from his bout with the flu. It took about a week before he was feeling well enough to go back to school. He wondered, though, what he could do to prevent ever getting the flu again. Are there ways that all of us can decrease our chances of coming into contact with the influenza viruses?

HOW ARE INFLUENZA VIRUSES SPREAD?

It is particularly difficult to prevent coming into contact with either cold or flu viruses after someone near you sneezes or coughs because the viruses pass easily through the air. Influenza is a respiratory disease and is very contagious. As can be seen in the photograph of the sneezing man (Figure 6.1), these tiny droplets can travel for long distances in the air and remain there to be inhaled by unsuspecting victims. These respiratory droplets can land on various surfaces and temporarily contaminate them, making it possible to pick up the virus by touch. During the winter months, we tend to stay inside more often, and major holidays bring together friends and family members from distant areas. Often these friends or relatives have spent several hours in airplanes with individuals who are infected with the influenza virus and may not show any immediate symptoms. With limited air replacement in the plane, dispersal of viruses into the air and on various surfaces promotes contact with the passengers. The viral frequent flyers strike again.

Figure 6.1 Why is it so important to cover your mouth when you sneeze? Each sneeze forces thousands of tiny, invisible respiratory droplets into the air. Influenza is a respiratory disease and can travel in these droplets. The sneeze in this picture was photographed at a very high speed to demonstrate how respiratory diseases can spread. (©Bettmann/Corbis)

Researchers have determined that children aged three to four are the first group to show signs of respiratory illnesses such as the flu. This will not come as a surprise to anyone who has a young relative. The researchers were from the Children's Hospital in Boston and the Harvard Medical School. Their work suggests that this age group is the driving force in new influenza epidemics. This data was strongly considered when The Centers for Disease Control and Prevention Advisory Committee on Immunization Practices (ACIP) recommended new immunization policies in 2007. The authors of the 2005 study had suggested that immunization policies should be based not only on who is at risk for the disease but also on those who are spreading the disease. This study seemed to confirm what many parents had noted for years.

More and more children are spending large amounts of time in preschool and daycare centers; these often become centers of infection due to the mingling of many young, vulnerable individuals. This 2005 study data, along with other simulations, suggests that the three- to four-year old age group serves as an indicator group. The study also showed that when compared with a database from the CDC, rates of flulike illnesses in children under five years of age served as an excellent predictor of pneumonia and influenza death rates in the general population. Given this new information, policy makers may have to reconsider who should receive the available vaccine in the case of a possible epidemic.[1]

Until 2007, immunization policies recommended that children over 23 months be vaccinated only if they had high-risk medical conditions. The 2007 recommendations of the CDC suggested that all hospitalized persons aged six months to four years be offered and strongly encouraged to receive the influenza vaccine before being discharged from the hospital.[2]

In February of 2008, ACIP voted to expand influenza vaccination recommendations to all children aged six months to 18 years. These recommendations add about 30 million children to the population to be vaccinated yearly. In addition, research presented at the annual meeting of the Pediatric Academic Societies (PAS) indicated that almost 11 million more children could be vaccinated if the vaccination was given near the beginning of the typical school year in August, when most children were already visiting their doctors. The study showed that starting vaccinations earlier and extending them later into the season increased the number of patients who complied with the two-dose regimen that was recommended for children younger than nine who had not been previously vaccinated.[3]

HOW TO KEEP THE FLU FROM CATCHING YOU

There are a number of simple measures that can reduce the likelihood of catching the flu. Common sense immediately suggests two basic ideas—avoidance and good personal hygiene. If you know that a person has the flu, avoid him or her. Talk to him or her on the telephone or send an e-mail but restrict your personal contact. Going to shopping malls, singing in the church or school choir or chorus, or joining your friends at an indoor music or sporting event all represent potential opportunities for the spread and dispersal of influenza viruses. It is important that newborn infants stay

COLD AND FLU IN ALASKA

Imagine sitting inside an airplane for four and one-half hours. This is not unusual on a cross-country trip. It was March in Homer, Alaska. It was freezing outside and therefore the pilot turned off the ventilation system, allowing the cabin to remain comfortable thanks to the body heat of the 49 passengers and five crew members. Among the passengers, a woman with a hacking cough was beginning to show the symptoms of the flu. The air was filled with her influenza viruses.

The plane finally took off and reached its final destination, Kodiak, Alaska, the next day. Within a day or two, 38 of the 54 persons who had been on that plane came down with the same strain of the influenza virus. The town's only doctor treated all of the sick patients. This 1977 episode represents the only documented incident of its type; an unplanned, controlled experiment with people who became sick from being confined in the same space with a particular virus.

away from crowds because their immune systems are not sufficiently developed to protect them.

Two major surfaces that should be cleaned regularly to prevent viral contamination and subsequent infection of people are telephones and door handles. Both are well-known sites for viral contaminants. There are a number of commercially available products that are effective in destroying viruses on various surfaces. You could also use a 10 percent solution of bleach to destroy the viruses.

Covering your mouth when you cough or sneeze has always been an effective way to minimize the spread of respiratory viruses. Recently the CDC has suggested that if you do not have a tissue you should cough or sneeze into your upper sleeve or elbow, not your hands. It is important to make sure that you wash your hands after you cough or sneeze. If you shake hands with someone who has the flu, if you use a telephone in a public place, if you open doors in public institutions or even at home, wash your hands! Most people wash their hands after they have changed a baby's diaper but not after they sneeze or cough. Research has shown that the simple act of washing your hands with soap and water for at least 15 seconds is the single most effective way of decreasing the spread of viruses. Waterless alcohol-based hand santizers are also effective. Try to avoid touching your nose, mouth, or eyes until you have had a chance to wash your hands, because these are portals that allow the virus to enter the body. Remember that you may become ill by coming into contact with someone currently infected with the influenza virus even though the person is not showing any symptoms. There is usually a delay of about 2 or 3 days between the time you become infected and when you begin to show symptoms. You may recall that Jim and his friends went to the concert Friday night in the packed Civic Center and by early Monday morning, Jim was showing his symptoms. An infected person may be contagious the day before symptoms first appear and continue to be contagious for another 3 to 5 days after the symptoms surface.

ANTIVIRAL MEDICATIONS

Recall that some of the medications used to fight the flu may also be given ahead of time to prevent getting the flu. These prescription drugs provide protection for individuals who cannot or have not been vaccinated. However, these medications should not be used as a substitute for vaccination.

Amantadine, also known as Symmetrel, was first approved for use as a preventive agent against influenza type A in

SOMETHING TO SNEEZE ABOUT

- Margaret Aimes opened the door to her home and began to sneeze, and she kept sneezing nonstop for more than 200 hours. She tried every known remedy to stop the sneezing. she finally stopped sneezing after she discovered that cheap cologne from her husband's friend was the cause.
- Not many people know that the very first copyrighted motion picture was made by one of Thomas Edison's assistants in 1894. The subject and title of the film were "The Sneeze," and it starred Fred Ott, an Edison employee. Mr. Ott was well known for his comical antics and ability to sneeze on cue.

   Pictures of Mr. Ott sneezing show the distribution of aerosol particles released from the nose and mouth. The sneeze leaves the nose and mouth at about 100 miles per hour. Sneezes are powerful because the muscles of the face, throat, and chest are all involved.
- Sneezes occur because nerve endings of the mucous membranes in the nose become irritated. The irritants may be dust, insects, bacteria, viruses, or almost any sort of foreign object. Even light may trigger an attack of sneezing.

1966. In 1976, its use was expanded to include adults and children older than one year of age. Rimantadine, or Flumadine, is related to amantadine and in 1993 was approved for use against influenza type A. Neither of these drugs works against influenza type B. In 2000, oseltamivir, or Tamiflu, was approved for use against both influenza types A and B virus for persons 13 and older. It is a useful medication if taken before exposure or even after exposure to the virus. This characteristic makes Tamiflu an important drug for individuals who continually find themselves surrounded by ill people during the flu season. In spite of the effectiveness of these antiviral agents, the best choice for prevention continues to be vaccination, especially considering the increased resistance to medications.

VACCINATION—WHO SHOULD BE VACCINATED?

There is nearly worldwide agreement about the need for people to be vaccinated against influenza. In the United States, the Centers for Disease Control and Prevention (CDC), the Food and Drug Administration (FDA), the National Institutes of Health (NIH), and various groups such as the American Lung Association (ALA) have issued guidelines as to who should and should not receive the annual vaccine. The Public Health Services of countries such as England, Australia, New Zealand, Germany, and Sweden, to name only a few, are also in agreement with the United States organizations.

Who should be vaccinated? It is clear that anyone who would like to decrease the chance of getting the flu should be vaccinated. The only exceptions are children less than six months of age and people who may be allergic to some component of the vaccine. Children who have been hospitalized should receive an influenza vaccination during their stay. Providing vaccinations for children who are hospitalized during flu season could reduce the number of hospital cases of influenza among young people by about 25 percent.

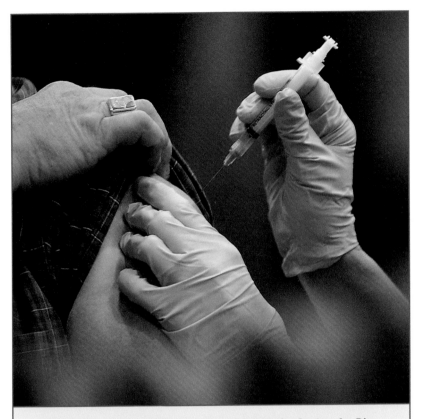

Figure 6.2 Vaccination is recommended by the Centers for Disease Control and Prevention (CDC) as an effective way to protect oneself from getting the flu. People who are at high risk for catching the flu are especially encouraged to get vaccinated. High-risk groups include the elderly, health care workers, people with certain diseases or disorders (diabetes, asthma, kidney or liver disease, impaired immune systems, for example). People who are allergic to any of component of the vaccine should talk with their doctors about alternative options. (© AP Images)

Since the year 2000, the CDC has recommended that anyone aged 50 or older should be vaccinated yearly. It is suggested that this group should also receive a pneumonia vaccine that would confer lifelong protection. Another group that should definitely be vaccinated is health care workers. Anyone who comes into contact with persons who are particularly susceptible to influenza should be vaccinated so that the risk of transmitting the disease to these people is decreased. Doctors, nurses, hospital personnel, nursing home employees, and those who work in chronic-care facilities and clinics are all obvious candidates. Home care nurses and volunteers, those who work in assisted living and other senior residences, as well as children and others who live with people at high risk for the flu also qualify.

Who is considered to be at high risk? On July 13, 2007, the CDC published its most recently revised influenza guidelines. The following list is a blending of the CDC recommendations and those of the American Academy of Pediatrics. In addition to healthy children aged six months through five years, the following individuals and groups should definitely be vaccinated:

- Anyone over the age of six months with underlying medical conditions, including those with:

  - Asthma or other chronic pulmonary diseases, such as cystic fibrosis (recommendation; evidence grade B)

  - Hemodynamically significant cardiac disease

  - Immunosuppressive disorders or who are undergoing immunosuppressive therapy

  - HIV infection

  - Sickle cell anemia and other hemoglobinopathies

  - Diseases requiring long-term aspirin therapy, such as juvenile idiopathic arthritis or Kawasaki disease

  - Chronic renal dysfunction

  - Chronic metabolic disease, such as diabetes mellitus

- Any condition that can compromise respiratory function or handling of secretions or can increase the risk of aspiration, such as cognitive dysfunction, spinal cord injuries, seizure disorders, or other neuromuscular disorders

- Household contacts and out-of-home caregivers of children younger than five years and children of all ages who are at risk. Immunization of close contacts of children younger than six months may be particularly important, because these infants cannot be immunized

- Children who required regular medical follow-up or hospitalization during the preceding year because of chronic metabolic diseases, such as diabetes mellitus; renal dysfunction; hemoglobinopathies; or immunodeficiency caused by medication or by HIV infection

- Any female who will be pregnant during influenza season

In addition, immunization is recommended for the following individuals to prevent transmission of influenza to those at risk, unless contraindicated[4]:

- Individuals five years of age and older

- Healthy contacts and caregivers of other children or adults at high risk of developing complications from influenza infection (recommendation; evidence grade B)

- Close contacts of immunosuppressed individuals (TIV only if severely immunosuppressed)

- Health care workers or volunteers

The National Foundation for Infectious Diseases (NFID) has outlined a number of strategies and tools that can be used to prevent influenza in diabetic patients. Dr. William Schaffner, vice president of NFID, presented a report entitled "Improving Influenza Vaccination Rates in Adults and Children with

Diabetes," to members of the CDC's Advisory Committee on Immunization Practices. The recommendations in this report included:

- Increasing influenza vaccine access and demand (e.g., establishing influenza vaccine-only clinics, offering extended office hours, undertaking consumer education)

- Overcoming practice-related barriers (e.g., updating standing orders, adding influenza vaccination to quality-care checklists)

- Recommending influenza vaccination through various channels (e.g., posters, postcards, e-mails) as well as for the entire office, including non-medical staff members

The importance of receiving an influenza vaccination is demonstrated by studies that show a 70 percent reduction in hospitalizations and deaths for diabetics who receive the shot. Additionally, there is a reduction by almost 80 percent in hospital admissions of children and adult diabetics who receive flu vaccinations.[5]

There are a few other groups that should strongly consider getting the flu vaccine. Viruses of all types are "frequent flyers" that fly for free on airlines that visit all parts of the globe. Travelers vary in their risk of exposure to influenza, depending on their travel destination and the time of the year they are traveling. Influenza occurs all year long in the tropics. In the temperate zone of the Southern Hemisphere, influenza normally occurs from April through September. In the Northern Hemisphere, October through March are the typical flu months. Based on this information, persons who plan to travel to the tropics or plan to travel with an organized tourist group at any time of the year should be sure to be vaccinated ahead of time. If a trip to the Southern Hemisphere is planned between April and September, the traveler should strongly consider the flu vaccine.

Community services personnel such as firemen and police officers provide important services that should not be disrupted by loss of personnel time. Teachers and religious leaders are surrounded by large numbers of people on a regular basis. Students at all levels of education, particularly those living in dormitory conditions, are prime candidates for contact with respiratory infectious agents. Individuals who attend large indoor rallies, convention events, sporting events, or musical gatherings are all susceptible. During epidemics, the risk of infection is present even at large outdoor parade rallies. All these individuals should be encouraged to receive the vaccine to minimize their chances of infection.

VACCINATION—WHO SHOULD NOT BE VACCINATED?

The injectable influenza vaccine is a suspension of inactivated influenza viruses. A vaccine is designed to stimulate the immune system to produce antibodies that will recognize particular microbes or viruses whenever they enter the host's body. This provides the host with long-term immunity against the specific microbe or virus. This type of immunity is known as active immunity.

The specific viruses thought to be needed for the year's vaccine are grown in eggs. There are three viral types used in the vaccine—two strains of type A and one strain of type B. The viruses are destroyed chemically and purified before the vaccine is completed. This type of vaccine is said to be made of inactivated viruses. The vaccine is continuously tested to ensure its purity, safety, and ability to stimulate the immune system of humans. Small amounts of egg protein may remain in the vaccine; therefore those individuals who may have allergic reactions to chicken eggs should consult their physicians about other options. Typical allergic reactions might include welts or hives, swelling of the tongue or lymph nodes, difficulty breathing, or, most dramatically, a loss in blood pressure resulting in shock.

People who are currently ill, particularly with upper respiratory tract infections, should wait until they have recovered before receiving the vaccine. In 1976, a limited number of people developed Guillain-Barre syndrome, a rare paralytic disorder, after being vaccinated. There has been no increase in risk of Guillain-Barre syndrome associated with vaccination since 1977.

The injectable influenza vaccine is made from viruses that are no longer active; therefore, you cannot become infected from the vaccine. The most common side effect is soreness at the site of the injection, which may last for 1 to 2 days. Less than one-third of the people who receive the shot have this reaction. Occasionally children may experience fever, fatigue, and muscle aches that start to occur 6 to 12 hours after the injection and last 1 to 2 days.

It takes about two weeks to build an antibody response that is protective. Occasionally, someone might catch the flu or develop symptoms from a flu virus they caught before they were vaccinated. Sometimes people think that the vaccine gave them the flu, but this is untrue.

SURVEILLANCE EFFORTS

In 1947, doctors and medical researchers suggested forming a worldwide watch (**surveillance**) for influenza outbreaks. The World Health Organization was founded in 1948 and given the responsibility for this international effort. WHO keeps a constant watch for outbreaks of influenza anywhere in the world. To accomplish this task, there are a series of 110 centers or "sentinel" laboratories located in 83 countries. Additionally, there are four major WHO Collaborating Centers for Virus Reference and Research. These major centers are located in Melbourne, Australia; Tokyo, Japan; London, England; and the CDC headquarters in Atlanta, Georgia.

This network of laboratories monitors activity through-out the world, and when a new outbreak of influenza occurs, these laboratories isolate the virus and send it and all available information to the closest WHO Center for Virus Reference and Research. The center then identifies the specific strain of virus involved in the outbreak. The centers are constantly iso-lating influenza viruses from humans and animals to determine which strains are currently in the environment. Consultations are held on a regular basis between the centers to review the information regarding which viruses are causing the current influenza episodes. This information makes it possible to

Table 6.1 Principles for Action on Pandemic and Seasonal Influenza

1. Establish a pandemic influenza vaccine master program.
2. Boost research and development and stockpiling of antibiotics and antivirals.
3. Improve diagnostic tools.
4. Improve the financial, legal, and regulatory environment for developing antiflu products.
5. Update plans for distributing and prioritizing antiflu supplies.
6. Improve seasonal influenza response.
7. Protect health care workers during a pandemic.
8. Build health care systems capable of responding to mass-casualty events.
9. Develop and test "community mitigation" measures.
10. Improve and coordinate surveillance.
11. Continue to strengthen leadership, international collaboration, and communication.
12. Commit funding for the long term.
Source: Infectious Disease Society of America

recommend which viral strains should be included in the vaccine composition for the next flu season. In May 2002, WHO adopted the content of a Global Agenda for the Management and Control of an Influenza Pandemic.

The CDC regularly releases updates on ways to deal with the possibility of a pandemic flu outbreak. Pre-planning is the best way to reduce both morbidity and mortality rates associated with such a worldwide outbreak. The CDC provides states, communities, businesses, and schools with a variety of tools to assist them in their planning.

Two broad categories of intervention strategies are suggested. Medical intervention involves using surveillance to identify flu cases and antiviral drugs to treat flu patients and reduce transmission of the viruses. The second category of intervention is more societal and is sometimes indicated as non-pharmaceutical. The use of school closures, voluntary quarantine, travel restrictions, and social distancing are some of the strategies involved.

Computer modeling suggests that without any of these interventions between 45 and 60 percent of the population will show the symptoms of influenza. Using even a minimal combination of the intervention strategies produced a reduction in the number of influenza cases of between 83 and 94 percent. Since a severe pandemic could kill up to two million Americans, it is critical that all health care personnel be vaccinated. It is also critical that the nation have a stockpile of vaccine readily available for its citizens.[6]

7
Dealing with Complications

For most people, including our friend Jim, a bout with the flu provides only an unpleasant memory. Of course Jim is a healthy, 18-year-old college freshman. He has no predisposing illness or conditions and does not fit into any high-risk groups. He lives at home, eats regularly, exercises, and does not smoke or drink. There are a number of individuals, however, who are at high risk for influenza. Those over 65 years of age are particularly susceptible.

Most of the complications associated with influenza involve the lower respiratory tract. The respiratory system starts at the nose and mouth and works down into the lungs. The origin of the complications may be bacterial, viral, or a combination of the two. For some individuals, existing chronic diseases may become worse. This is especially true for those suffering from cardiopulmonary diseases.

TYPICAL SYMPTOMS

Influenza viruses are spread by way of respiratory droplets, sometimes known as aerosols. The virus particles bind to cells of the respiratory epithelium by means of the hemagglutinin (HA) proteins. The cells of the respiratory epithelium, specifically the simple ciliated columnar and the pseudostratified ciliated columnar epithelium, are filled with viral receptors. As the newly formed viruses are preparing to leave the host cell, the protein neuraminidase (NA) helps to separate the viruses from each other and the host cell membrane, thus aiding the infectious process by releasing virus particles that have been bound by the mucus present on the surface of epithelial cells.

The usual symptoms of influenza appear after a typical incubation period of about 48 hours. A rapidly developing fever that may reach over 101 degrees Fahrenheit is matched by a splitting headache. The fever is usually present and lasts about 3 days. There is usually also shivering, a dry raspy cough, fatigue, and muscular aches and pains. Some individuals become sensitive to light, but this is not common to all. Influenza type B infections are similar to those caused by influenza type A, but infections with influenza type C usually go unnoticed or are very mild in nature.

COMPLICATIONS—RESPIRATORY

Because influenza viruses normally replicate in the lower, warmer, respiratory tract, the tissues of the lung often become swollen and inflamed. After the viruses have invaded the columnar epithelium, they begin replication, which reaches its peak 1 to 3 days after that initial infection. Damage occurs almost immediately as cells start to die and swelling and inflammation begin, often spreading to the bronchioles (extensions of the bronchi) and alveoli (lung or air sacs). This inflammatory response creates slight damage to the lungs, but they usually heal within a few weeks. The epithelial cells normally begin their recovery within a week, but restoration of full function for the cilia and for mucus production may take 2 weeks. Mucus is produced by modified epithelium called goblet or mucous cells. Cilia are protein microtubules that extend through cell membranes and serve to sweep mucus-laden materials upward so they can be removed from the body. A variety of conditions and agents, including smoking and influenza, may damage or depress the cilia and prevent their proper functioning.

In those individuals with a depressed, impaired, or slowed immune system, complications may arise. The very young and the very old often have a slower than normal immune response.

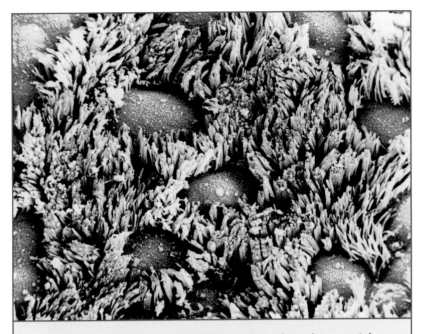

Figure 7.1 Cells in the wall of the trachea, shown here, contain hemagglutinin proteins. The airborne virus particles enter the respiratory system and bind to these proteins. A protein called neuraminidase helps the viruses to separate from one another, effectively releasing more particles into the body. (© Michael Gabridge/Custom Medical Stock Photo)

The most common and potentially the most severe of the complications leads to pneumonia. Pneumonia is a general term for an inflammatory disease of the lungs. This inflammation may lead to tissue damage. At this point, the damaged cells release their fluid contents into the lung area, further decreasing surface area for exchange of oxygen and carbon dioxide gases.

Pneumonia related to influenza may have a bacterial or a viral origin. Bacterial pneumonia is considered to be the most common form, pure viral pneumonia the least common form, and a combination of both lies somewhere in between. Many of the bacteria responsible for bacterial pneumonia are found as part of the normal flora of the nose and throat. When the influenza virus damages and weakens the lungs and the cilia in the trachea, these bacteria are able to descend into the lungs. Loss of ciliary function prevents mucus from being swept upward and being removed from the body. This results in what is sometimes called a "superinfection," with bacteria that are part of the normal flora becoming opportunistic and creating damage to the host cells. The three bacterial species mentioned most frequently in association with influenza-related pneumonia are *Staphylococcus aureus, Streptococcus pneumoniae,* and *Haemophilus influenzae.* Patients with bacterial pneumonia usually respond favorably to treatment with antibiotics. Sometimes antibiotics are not effective because of bacterial resistance to the antibiotic. In patients with existing heart or lung disease, circulatory failure may occur. If the immune system is severely depressed, toxins released by the bacteria may overwhelm the patient, leading to a lack of oxygen being carried to the body or to toxic shock syndrome. Toxic shock syndrome is caused by toxins released by specific strains of *Staphylococcus aureus.* Recent evidence suggests that the genetic information on how to make these toxins was provided by viruses that infected the *Staphyloccus* bacteria.

Worsening of an already existing condition known as COPD (chronic obstructive pulmonary disease) is not uncommon with influenza infections. This COPD syndrome, usually caused by smoking, may involve a combination of conditions, including chronic bronchitis, asthma, emphysema, and cystic fibrosis. Any significant obstruction of the air passages leads to coughing, wheezing, and painful breathing, known as dyspnea.

COMPLICATIONS OTHER THAN RESPIRATORY

Some of the other complications related to influenza may involve the heart and circulatory system, the muscles, and the central nervous system. Although cardiac complications have occurred in apparently healthy young adults, the bulk of cases involve older persons with pre-existing cardiopulmonary disease. A common cardiac complication in older persons is atrial fibrillation, a condition in which the contractions of the right and left atria or auricles of the heart are out of rhythm and often twitch. This usually leads to lack of pumping action by this part of the heart. Even in a strong heart, atrial fibrillation may reduce pumping action by 20 to 30 percent. **Pericarditis**, inflammation of the membrane surrounding the heart, and myocarditis, inflammation of the heart muscle itself, have been associated with influenza.

Although a certain amount of aches and muscular pains are common in influenza, some doctors have reported leg pains and muscle tenderness that may last up to 5 days in children. This muscular involvement for children has been related to infection by influenza B virus. Inflammation of muscle fibers is known as myositis.

Cases of encephalitis, inflammation of the tissues of the brain, have also been reported and can be severe. In children, another complication of influenza is otitis media, an infection of the middle ear which, if not treated quickly, can lead to rupturing of the eardrum. The infection is caused by bacteria, and the treatment may include draining pus from the middle ear. The bacteria pass from the nasopharyngeal region into the eustachian tube. Since children have shorter eustachian tubes, they tend to be more susceptible to middle ear infections. In addition, because influenza decreases the flow of mucus away from the tube, more bacteria are likely to be in the area. One last condition to mention is Reye's syndrome, a previously mentioned condition that is more a complication of the attempt to control fever by taking aspirin products. Although rare, it is an important complication in young children and adolescents. As many as 10–40 percent of those affected may die, and many survivors may suffer serious nervous system damage.

The CDC suggests that, in an average year, complications from influenza may lead to approximately 36,000 deaths and

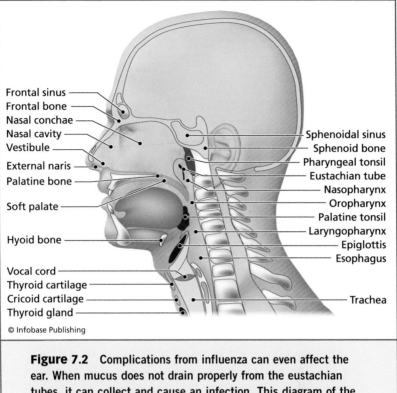

Frontal sinus
Frontal bone
Nasal conchae
Nasal cavity
Vestibule
External naris
Palatine bone

Soft palate

Hyoid bone

Vocal cord
Thyroid cartilage
Cricoid cartilage
Thyroid gland

Sphenoidal sinus
Sphenoid bone
Pharyngeal tonsil
Eustachian tube
Nasopharynx
Oropharynx
Palatine tonsil
Laryngopharynx
Epiglottis
Esophagus

Trachea

© Infobase Publishing

Figure 7.2   Complications from influenza can even affect the ear. When mucus does not drain properly from the eustachian tubes, it can collect and cause an infection. This diagram of the head shows some of the areas that can be affected by influenza, including the eustachian tube, the tonsils, and the nasopharynx (nasopharyngeal region).

over 100,000 hospital cases nationwide. Flu is the fifth leading cause of death of the elderly.

HOW THE BODY DEALS WITH INFLUENZA

We begin by studying the body's defenses in general and then look in greater depth at how these defenses deal with invasion by viruses such as influenza. This first group of defenses is not selective and is designed to keep out any and all invaders and thus the members of this group are usually called nonspecific defenses. The first line of the body's defense is the unbroken skin and the mucous membranes lining the respiratory, gastrointestinal, and urogenital tracts. In addition, there are mechanical, cellular, and biochemical mechanisms that act along these surface membranes. As has been discussed, influenza viruses kill some of the cells lining the throat and destroy or inactivate the cilia on their surfaces. This damage to the cilia and to mucus production along the upper respiratory tract allows bacteria to invade the lower respiratory tract and cause pneumonia.

Another nonspecific response occurs when the skin or other cells are damaged or penetrated. This response is known as **inflammation**. The process follows a standard series of events, well known to most people. This sequence occurs no matter what the cause or how frequent the invasion. The damaged area becomes red (inflamed) and begins to feel warm to the touch. Soon the area is swollen and begins to hurt. Within a few days the swelling, heat, and pain begin to subside. After a few more days one may be unaware of the previously damaged site. Most of these symptoms are the result of blood flow into the affected area. Increased blood flow leads to the redness, heat, and swelling but also brings two major types of white blood cells (WBCs) to the area, the **neutrophils** and the monocytes.

Monocytes have the ability to change their shape and increase their activity level when they move from the bloodstream into the tissues. These modified monocytes are known as **macrophages**, literally giant eating machines. These WBCs are important for several reasons. They begin to engulf, through the process of **phagocytosis**, **pathogenic** organisms or debris from damaged cells. Neutrophils are active for 24 to 48 hours and then die. Monocytes or macrophages may remain in the tissues for several weeks to aid in the repair efforts. They may also release enzymes that keep the inflammatory process going. Unfortunately, this may lead to further tissue damage

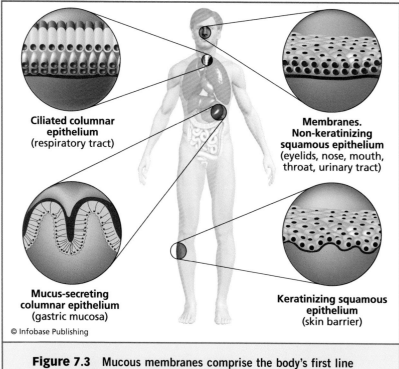

Ciliated columnar
epithelium
(respiratory tract)

Membranes.
Non-keratinizing
squamous epithelium
(eyelids, nose, mouth,
throat, urinary tract)

Mucus-secreting
columnar epithelium
(gastric mucosa)

Keratinizing squamous
epithelium
(skin barrier)

© Infobase Publishing

Figure 7.3   Mucous membranes comprise the body's first line of defense. They prevent foreign microorganisms from entering the body. They are considered a nonspecific defense because they keep out all types of invaders. The diagram above shows some of the locations of mucous membranes in the human body.

and require the use of anti-inflammatory medications such as aspirin. Other chemicals released by macrophages stimulate monocytes to convert into macrophages, thus increasing their numbers. Macrophages also release a protein called interleukin-1, which signals the brain to increase the temperature in the region, causing a fever. The increased temperature often increases the blood flow into the area.

Inflammation is designed to eliminate the invader and repair the damaged cells or tissue. The WBCs move into the damaged area. Neutrophils are followed several hours later by

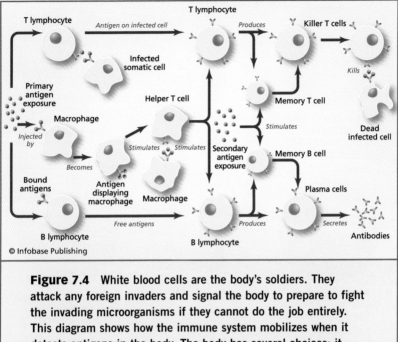

T lymphocyte

T lymphocyte

Antigen on infected cell

Produces

Killer T cells

Infected somatic cell

Kills

Primary antigen exposure

Helper T cell

Memory T cell

Macrophage

Injected by

Stimulates

Stimulates

Secondary antigen exposure

Memory B cell

Stimulates

Dead infected cell

Becomes

Bound antigens

Antigen displaying macrophage

Macrophage

Plasma cells

Free antigens

Produces

Secretes

B lymphocyte

B lymphocyte

Antibodies

© Infobase Publishing

Figure 7.4 White blood cells are the body's soldiers. They attack any foreign invaders and signal the body to prepare to fight the invading microorganisms if they cannot do the job entirely. This diagram shows how the immune system mobilizes when it detects antigens in the body. The body has several choices: it can send T lymphocytes to attack the infected cell, ingest the antigens using macrophages, or send B lymphocytes to bind to the antigens.

macrophages, which adhere to edges of the damaged tissue. From invasion to completed repairs usually takes 8 to 10 days.

Viral invasion of cells causes the cells to produce a group of proteins known as **interferons**. This response is independent of, and thus nonspecific to, the type of virus that has invaded the cell. The production of these interferon proteins acts to inhibit the replication process of the viruses. The ability of the invaded cell to reproduce is inhibited, and a group of cells called **natural killer** (NK) cells are impacted. NK cells have the ability to recognize and lyse (break down) cells that have become infected with viruses. The NK cells release proteins that rupture the membranes of infected cells and then poison the cells with additional toxins that they produce. Researchers have not clearly identified the specific receptors that the NK cells are able to recognize. NK cells can act immediately and thus are effective early in the development of the viral infection. Their ability to destroy infected cells helps to limit the spread of the viral invasion. Ironically, most of the symptoms of the flu, such as headache, aching muscles, fever, and exhaustion, are caused by the release of the body's defensive chemicals, particularly interferon.

Scientists recently discovered a type of immune response that is specific to the lungs. It is thought that this type of immunity developed as a way of reducing inflammation damage. The alveola, tiny pockets of lung tissue involved in gaseous exchange, are protected from invading microbes or particles such as dust or fibers by a type of white blood cell known as alveolar macrophages.

Macrophages are involved in the inflammatory response throughout the body. According to Eyal Raz, a researcher who wrote about alveolar macrophages in the science journal *Immunity*, "Alveolar macrophages are unique among macrophages in the body, because their activation is inhibited by TGFb, a compound expressed in the lung by epithelial cells. Because the microenvironment of the alveola is a delicate one, it would be damaged if the macrophage immune system was in a constant battle-ready status."[1] Inflammation of this type is often seen in lung diseases like asthma.

To offset this potential problem, the macrophage is kept "asleep" in its normal state and "awakened" when it needs to confront invading microorganisms. After its successful engagement with the microbes, it is put back to sleep.

According to Raz, figuring out how this immune mechanism works gives scientists clues about how to possibly prolong the activation of alveolar macrophages. This knowledge in turn could lead to finding ways to fight other infections of the lower airways, including new strains of influenza.

Recovery from a viral infection such as influenza takes several days and is attributable mainly to a new class of protein molecules created specifically to destroy the virus. Viruses, bacteria, foreign proteins, or molecules from almost any source other than the body itself are known as antigens (Ag). When cells of the immune system recognize these alien cells or molecules, they begin to mobilize various chemicals and cells against these specific antigens. This type of defense represents a *specific response* because a unique Ag will cause production of molecules specifically directed against that antigen.

A third type of WBC known as a **lymphocyte** is involved in the specific immune response. About one trillion lymphocytes are involved, and they are divided into two major categories known as the **B lymphocytes** and the **T lymphocytes**. B lymphocytes mature mainly in the bone marrow, and when they recognize antigens, the B cells are modified into short-lived cells that produce millions of copies of a single type of protein. The modified cells are called **plasma cells,** and the protein produced is known as antibody (Ab) or immunoglobulin. The Ab has been produced to act against a specific antigen. The joining of Ag-Ab results in the antigen's being tagged for destruction.

In order to recognize and react to specific antigens, both B and T cells have specific receptor glycoproteins embedded in their cell membranes. After recognition and contact with the foreign invader, a series of chemicals, usually proteins, are released to communicate this information to other parts of the immune system. Finally, action is taken. B cells are converted to plasma cells, which produce antibodies (Ab) specific to this foreign invader. Antibodies are released into the body fluids or humors. This type of specific immunity is sometimes referred to as **humoral immunity** or **antibody-mediated immunity.**

There are five different types of antibodies or immunoglobulins (Ig) that are produced in response to recognition of a specific antigen. The types are designated IgA, IgD, IgE, IgG, and IgM. The type of Ig produced depends on the target site in the

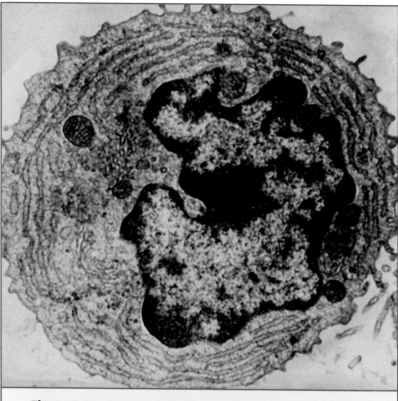

Figure 7.5a Plasma cells produce antibodies that act against specific antigens. Plasma cells are mature B lymphocytes and have special receptor glycoproteins that recognize specific antigens. When a plasma cell finds a cell containing an antigen (i.e. one that has been invaded by a virus) that matches its antibody, it will attempt to kill that cell. (Courtesy CDC)

body, genetic variability of the host, type of antigen involved, and whether or not this is the first time that the antigen has been recognized by the host. IgG antibody is found in the secretions of the lower respiratory tract, whereas IgA is the dominant form found in secretions of the upper respiratory tract. Both are involved in immunity against influenza. These circulating antibodies are the primary protection against viral infections or attachment to the host cell. From a functional standpoint, the most effective type of antibodies are those that can bind to the hemagglutinin protein in the envelope of the influenza virus. This prevents attachment and penetration of the virus. If antibodies are provided after an infection has already occurred, the number of infectious viral particles released from the cells is usually reduced. The major benefit of vaccination is its priming effect on antibody development. Without vaccination, the immune system must wait until cells have been infected and viruses are present in large enough numbers to be detected. By that time one is sick, and it will be 3 to 5 days before there are sufficient antibodies to slow the invasion.

T lymphocytes are capable of regulating the entire immune system and its responses. T cells can turn on or off some or all parts of the system. This regulation is part of the body's homeostatic controls. T cells interact with larger targets, such as cell surfaces. This type of immunity is known as **cell-mediated immunity** (CMI). There are a number of subpopulations of T cells. **Helper T cells** are often mentioned in a discussion of AIDS. Helper T cells are also called CD4 or T4 cells or lymphocytes. They serve as traffic police and cheerleaders of the immune system. When antigens (Ag) are recognized and interleukin-1 (IL-1) is released by the macrophages, helper T cells produce a protein known as interleukin-2 (IL-2). IL-2 activates B cells to produce Ab specific to the Ag. It also activates other T cells called **cytotoxic T cells** which, together with NK cells, attack infected cells. The helper T cells also activate neutrophils and macrophages and stimulate release of WBCs from the bone marrow. This is only a small sample of what the helper cells are involved in. It should be easy to see that any conditions that diminish the ability of the helper T cells to do their job have a major effect on the entire spectrum of immune responses. The HIV targets the helper T cell.

Most people are aware of one type of cell-mediated immunity that involves rejection of transplanted organs. T cells produce a series of chemicals called **cytokines** or **lymphokines**.

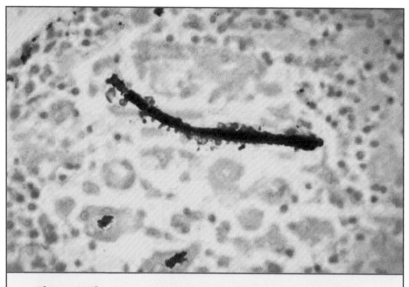

Figure 7.5b Macrophages attack foreign invaders. An asbestos fiber is lodged in the lung tissue is surrounded by macrophages, which are stained pink in this photo. Iron complexes, stained blue, also surround the asbestos fiber. The macrophages will attempt to engulf and break down the foreign body. (Courtesy CDC/Dr. Edwin P. Ewing Jr.)

These cytokines bind to specific receptors on the targeted cells and can carry out a multitude of functions, depending on the type of cytokine. Some are involved in the inflammatory process, some directly destroy targeted cells, and others serve as chemical messengers directing cellular traffic or promoting cellular growth and activity. One of the earliest cytokines to be discovered was interferon, mentioned earlier.

This RCA sequence (Recognition, Communication, Action), or some version of it, constitutes the most common immune response. Thus, a strain of influenza will cause infected individuals to produce Ab specific for that strain and set into motion a cascade of chemical messages that involve many segments of the body.

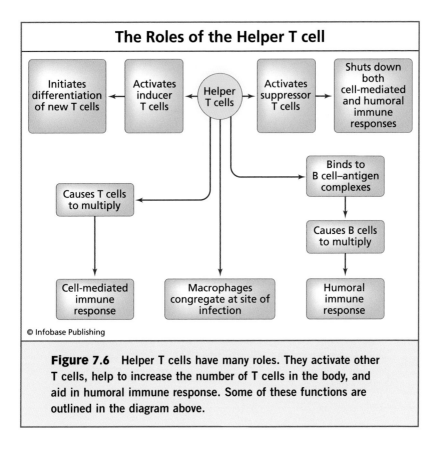

The Roles of the Helper T cell

© Infobase Publishing

Figure 7.6 Helper T cells have many roles. They activate other T cells, help to increase the number of T cells in the body, and aid in humoral immune response. Some of these functions are outlined in the diagram above.

Scientists from Emory University School of Medicine in Atlanta, Georgia, and the Oklahoma Medical Research Foundation in Oklahoma City have developed a technique that will produce large quantities of human monoclonal antibodies (mAbs) against influenza virus strains. The technique they have developed will be useful against other diseases as well.

Human monoclonal antibodies are produced from a single antibody-producing cell that has the capability of creating identical, highly specific, infection-fighting proteins (the antibodies) rapidly and in prodigious numbers. The new technique produces the mAbs in a shorter time than the usual 2 to 3 weeks by using a subset of immune system cells called antibody secreting plasma cells (ASCs). These mAbs bind tightly to the virus strains found in the seasonal vaccines and thus should bind tightly to the viruses that are being targeted by these vaccines. Dr. Anthony Fauci, director of the National Institutes of Health's National Institute of Allergy and Infectious Diseases (NIAID), commented that this new technique "opens the way to producing mAbs that potentially could be used diagnostically or therapeutically not only for influenza but for other infectious diseases as well."[2] This advance allows for a small amount of blood, perhaps the equivalent of a few tablespoons, to rapidly generate disease-fighting mAbs as soon as the disease outbreak is noted in the population.

The significance of the monoclonal antibody technique is related to the ability of influenza viruses to cause repeated infections. By constantly changing their structure through mutation of the hemagglutinin (HA) and neuraminidase (NA) surface glycoproteins, the host body is stimulated to make new antibodies. Since it may take a week or more for a host to produce a sufficient supply of new antibodies, having a ready supply of antibodies in the form of the mAbs will provide a means of reducing the spread of the disease and eliminating the possibility of an epidemic or pandemic. As the new strain of virus is identified, mAbs can be produced to serve as both diagnostic tools and therapeutic weapons.[3]

We have only scratched the surface of the intricate nature of the interactions involved in providing protection to the cells and the organism. There are numerous excellent texts and monographs that can provide an even deeper understanding of the immune system and its mechanisms. What is clear is that, in the case of infection by influenza viruses, a fully functioning immune system will allow the disease to run its course within a few days. Avoiding the disease and its symptoms requires a preemptive attack on your part—namely, vaccination.

8

Avian Flu: Not Just for the Birds

Consider a potential population mortality of over 100 million. That is nearly one-third of the population of the United States. According to the World Health Organization, it is the estimate of the number of people who could die in the next human influenza pandemic. The influenza viruses that have prompted these estimates are the highly pathogenic avian influenza (HPAI) viruses of the H5N1 subtype. Avian influenza virus is classified as either low pathogenic avian influenza (LPAI), which causes mild or asymptomatic infections in poultry, or HPAI, which causes severe disease and is lethal to chickens.

Since the current human mortality rate for avian influenza is about 60 percent, it is easy to see that health care personnel and facilities would quickly become overwhelmed. WHO considers the avian influenza A/(H5N1) virus a public health menace with pandemic potential.

As of April 30, 2008, there had been 382 confirmed human cases and 241 human deaths caused by H5N1 influenza virus. These represent only laboratory-confirmed cases. The actual numbers of unreported and unconfirmed cases would be expected to be much higher and mortality rates are therefore difficult to project.

Most of the human cases have been associated with infected poultry, primarily chickens and ducks. In an effort to prevent transmission of the virus, infected poultry herds have been extensively culled. The numbers killed are over 100 million. In addition to chickens and ducks, numerous other species have become part of the transmission problem. Included are

Table 8.1   Cumulative Number of Confirmed Human Cases of Avian Influenza A/(H5N1) Reported to WHO

Country	2003 cases	2003 deaths	2004 cases	2004 deaths	2005 cases	2005 deaths	2006 cases	2006 deaths	2007 cases	2007 deaths	2008 cases	2008 deaths	Total cases	Total deaths
Azerbaijan	0	0	0	0	0	0	8	5	0	0	0	0	8	5
Cambodia	0	0	0	0	4	4	2	2	1	1	0	0	7	7
China	1	1	0	0	8	5	13	8	5	3	3	3	30	20
Djibouti	0	0	0	0	0	0	1	0	0	0	0	0	1	0
Egypt	0	0	0	0	0	0	18	10	25	9	7	3	50	22
Indonesia	0	0	0	0	20	13	55	45	42	37	15	12	132	107
Iraq	0	0	0	0	0	0	3	2	0	0	0	0	3	2
Lao People's Democratic Republic	0	0	0	0	0	0	0	0	2	2	0	0	2	2
Myanmar	0	0	0	0	0	0	0	0	1	0	0	0	1	0
Nigeria	0	0	0	0	0	0	0	0	1	1	0	0	1	1
Pakistan	0	0	0	0	0	0	0	0	3	1	0	0	3	1
Thailand	0	0	17	12	5	2	3	3	0	0	0	0	25	17
Turkey	0	0	0	0	0	0	12	4	0	0	0	0	12	4
Vietnam	3	3	29	20	61	19	0	0	8	5	5	5	106	52
Total	4	4	46	32	98	43	115	79	88	59	30	23	381	240

Total number of cases includes number of deaths. • WHO reports only laboratory-confirmed cases. • All dates refer to onset of illness.

Source: http://www.who.int/csr/disease/avian_influenza/country/cases_table_2008_04_17/en/index.html. Updated April 17, 2008.

swans, geese, turkeys, gulls, cats, leopards, tigers, dogs, pigs, horses, mink, stone martens, and ferrets.

TRANSMISSION OF AVIAN FLU

Human infection with A/(H5N1) virus was first reported in Hong Kong in 1997. This avian-to-human transmission caused 18 cases of infection and six deaths. The virus migrated from Southeast Asia to the Middle East, coastal Africa, Europe, and the former Soviet Union states over the next decade. To date avian influenza has been identified in 46 countries. A recent report from China suggests that the virus is showing signs of mutating. A number of sources have suggested that the spread of the virus from China into Europe and Russia can be traced to the migratory flight patterns of infected waterfowl.[1,2] Researchers hope they will be able to increase their prediction rate regarding any new outbreaks by looking at available data in a number of new ways.

The avian influenza virus is spread through the fecal-oral route, airborne transmission, and through contaminated water involving aquatic birds. Birds excrete the virus in their fecal matter. As the feces dry out and become pulverized, they aerosolize and are easily inhaled. Humans traditionally acquire the disease by having close contact with the live infected animals. Avian flu is not a foodborne virus, so eating cooked chicken or duck will not cause the disease, although slaughterhouse personnel are at increased risk. The greatest concern is that infected humans will easily pass the disease on to other humans. So far, there have been a limited number of human-to-human transmissions, and all of the cases were among close family members.

THE SUGARS THAT BIND

Whether an influenza virus can infect a human depends on the structure of a protein on the surface of the virus being capable of attaching to a specific receptor on the surface of cells of the respiratory tract. This host receptor is a combination of simple sugars and protein and is called a glycoprotein. In humans, the receptors possess a particular chemical linkage that is known as alpha 2,6. In birds the receptors are slightly different and known as alpha 2,3. Avian viruses bind to receptors in the intestinal epithelial cells. The upper respiratory tract of humans—the main infection site for influenza viruses—is populated by receptors of the alpha 2,6 type. The lower respiratory tract in humans has an abundance of alpha 2,3 receptors and could thus become an infection site if large quantities of the virus were present. Our current scientific understanding suggested that a genetic mutation could makes it possible for the virus to bind to alpha 2,6 receptors instead of alpha 2,3 receptors. It is thought that this type of mutation is the most likely reason that avian viruses were able to infect humans.

A recent study by a group from the Massachusetts Institute of Technology (MIT) has added new scientific understanding to the mechanism of attachment of viral and host cell receptors. The researchers have shown that the largest factor in allowing the attachment is the shape of the sugar receptors in the human lung cells, not the specific linkage. The alpha 2,6 receptors of humans come in two shapes. One looks like a mushroom cap or umbrella, and the other looks like a cone ready to be filled with ice cream. At the present time, bird influenza viruses attach only to these cone-shaped receptors and not the umbrella-shaped ones, which are more prevalent. In order to become pandemic, it would seem that the viruses would need to mutate to a form that could use the umbrella-shaped receptors. These new findings from the MIT study show that our previous understandings do not adequately explain how viruses evolve to infect humans. The MIT group said that this discovery will provide new ways to monitor the bird flu virus as well as develop therapeutic techniques and materials for both avian and seasonal flu.[3]

ANTIGENIC SHIFT

Another concern for influenza researchers is the problem of antigenic shift. Antigenic shift is the major genetic change resulting in the emergence of a strain in humans with a different HA or NA surface protein. Antigenic shift can happen in three ways:

Antigenic Shift 1 (Reassortment)

- A duck or other aquatic bird passes a bird strain of influenza A to an intermediate host such as a pig.

- A person passes a human strain of influenza A to the same pig.

- When the viruses infect the same cell, the genes from the bird strain mix with genes from the human strain to yield a new strain.

- The new strain can spread from the intermediate host to humans.

Antigenic Shift 2 (Direct Transmission Between Species)

- Without undergoing genetic change, a bird strain of influenza A can jump directly from a duck or other aquatic bird to humans.

Antigenic Shift 3 (Indirect Transmission Between Species)

- Without undergoing genetic change, a bird strain of influenza A can jump directly from a duck or other aquatic bird to an intermediate animal host and then to humans.

- Antigenic shift can also occur in the human population when an older strain re-emerges, as when the Russian Flu (H1N1) re-emerged in 1977.

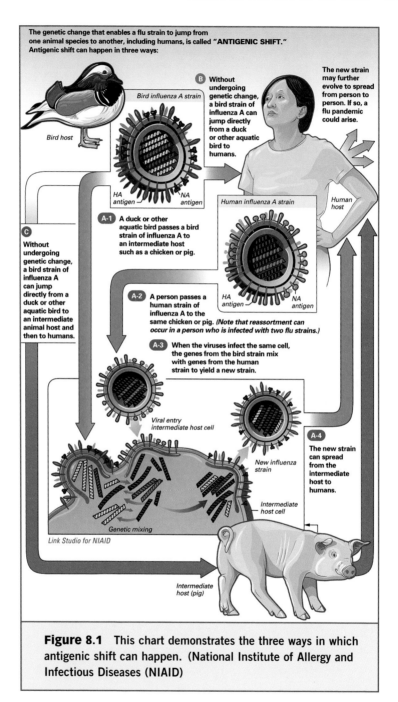

The genetic change that enables a flu strain to jump from one animal species to another, including humans, is called "ANTIGENIC SHIFT." Antigenic shift can happen in three ways:

Bird host

Bird influenza A strain

B Without undergoing genetic change, a bird strain of influenza A can jump directly from a duck or other aquatic bird to humans.

The new strain may further evolve to spread from person to person. If so, a flu pandemic could arise.

HA antigen

NA antigen

Human influenza A strain

Human host

A-1 A duck or other aquatic bird passes a bird strain of influenza A to an intermediate host such as a chicken or pig.

C Without undergoing genetic change, a bird strain of influenza A can jump directly from a duck or other aquatic bird to an intermediate animal host and then to humans.

A-2 A person passes a human strain of influenza A to the same chicken or pig. *(Note that reassortment can occur in a person who is infected with two flu strains.)*

HA antigen

NA antigen

A-3 When the viruses infect the same cell, the genes from the bird strain mix with genes from the human strain to yield a new strain.

Viral entry intermediate host cell

New influenza strain

A-4 The new strain can spread from the intermediate host to humans.

Intermediate host cell

Genetic mixing

Link Studio for NIAID

Intermediate host (pig)

Figure 8.1 This chart demonstrates the three ways in which antigenic shift can happen. (National Institute of Allergy and Infectious Diseases (NIAID)

After an antigenic shift has occurred, the new strain may further evolve to spread easily from person to person. If so, a flu pandemic could arise. The conditions indicated by Antigenic Shift 1 involving human and bird flu viruses mixing together in an intermediate such as a pig are possible because the tracheal cells of the pig contain both alpha 2,6 and alpha 2,3 receptors. This makes it easier for coinfection and mixing of the viruses leading to possible new virus types. These new types would not have been seen previously by the human immune system and could quickly and easily lead to epidemic situations. Pigs were thought to be the reservoirs for the 1918 pandemic and were also considered as a major reservoir again in 1976–1977. This latter event led to a mass immunization effort in the United States.

WHAT CAN WE DO? WHAT ARE WE DOING?

These two questions are linked. One of the things we can do is find ways to rapidly determine if poultry are infected with the H5N1 virus. Research teams at the University of Arkansas and at Georgia Tech have developed inexpensive biosensors to detect the presence of avian influenza virus H5N1 from poultry in fewer than 30 minutes. These instruments are portable and available for field studies. They are easily connected to laptop computers for data acquisition and analysis. The key idea is that rapid detection can lead to a rapid response for eradication, quarantine, and vaccination.

To eliminate drinking water as a potential source of transmission of influenza viruses to poultry as well as to humans, researchers developed experiments using chlorinated water. Chlorine is the most common form of water disinfection, but government reports have only dealt with enteric or intestinal forms of viruses. The results of the study show that avian influenza viruses are also easily inactivated by standard chlorination.[4]

"Be prepared" is a common motto. Since the early 2000s WHO, the CDC, medical groups, state governments, and national agencies such as the Department of Health and Human Services and the Department of Homeland Security, and even other countries' governments, have worked together to develop emergency response plans.

Vaccine development and distribution are also important in dealing with avian influenza and its pandemic potential. As of 2008 there is no commercially available vaccine designed to protect against H5N1. Ironically, no vaccine against a pandemic virus can be produced until the new pandemic virus arrives on the scene and is identified and characterized.

Various government agencies are working together to develop vaccines based on the current strains of H5N1. While some of the current prescription medications have shown to be effective against the avian form of the flu, many of the human and avian strains are becoming resistant to some of these medications.

In spite of all the remaining concerns, it is clear that the world is now better prepared to deal with a potential pandemic. Emergency response plans have been written. Laboratories have gotten better and faster at identifying influenza. Potentially infected poultry are quickly culled, suspected patients are treated with oseltamivir, and the origin of their disease symptoms is rapidly traced. Progress on producing vaccines has allowed for developers to use smaller amounts of material to elicit a response. Some scientists have suggested that H5 viruses have been around for more than 100 years and not caused any pandemics. Whether that will continue is unknown. What is known is that we need to persist in our efforts to find answers to the questions posed by the threat of avian influenza.

9

What May the Future Bring? The Past and Future Concerns

The great Spanish philosopher George Santayana reminded us that "Those who cannot remember the past are condemned to repeat it." With this thought in mind, we revisit the history of influenza in order to learn from it.

THE EARLY YEARS

Antonie van Leeuwenhoek (Figure 9.1) discovered microorganisms in the late 1600s with his simple microscope-like device. Discovery of these previously unseen organisms led to speculation that they might be the cause of disease. During the 1700s, techniques were developed and refined that provided protection against some diseases by stimulating an individual's immune system. These techniques, including vaccinations, were based on earlier observations made by the Romans and also the Chinese that individuals who recover from some diseases do not contract the same disease again.

A virus was still thought of as a chemical poison or toxin through the 1700s, not a distinct structure. Much of our understanding was about to change as we moved into the mid-to-late 1800s. By the 1800s, all major trading routes and contacts had been established. Europe, Asia, and North America maintained continuous, although slow, contact through their

Figure 9.1 Using a simple magnifying device, Antonie von Leeuwenhoek, pictured here, discovered microorganisms in the late 1600s. His "microscope" magnified up to 200 times, much more than previous magnifying devices. His discovery led to the hypothesis that microorganisms might be the cause of disease. (© Bettmann/Corbis)

shipping trade. Late in 1829 an epidemic of influenza started in Asia. By January of 1831 it had reached Indonesia. At the same time, during the winter of 1830–1831, the disease appeared in

Russia and began to spread westward. By November of 1831 it had reached the United States.

The Southern Hemisphere was not free of the disease either. Following a visit to New Zealand in 1826 by a British ship, a serious outbreak of the disease occurred. The native population was highly susceptible because they had had no previous contact with the disease. A more severe epidemic broke out at the end of 1838. It seemed that everyone in the northern part of the island was affected. The elderly and those in poor health died in large numbers. Both New Zealand and Australia reported a large number of cases of flu between 1852 and 1860.

In the summer of 1889 a pandemic (worldwide epidemic) began in central Asia. Following a number of trade routes, the disease spread north to Russia, east to China, and west to Europe. England was invaded by the disease during the first week of 1890. At the peak of the epidemic in 1891 and 1892, more than 4,000 people, mostly infants and the elderly, died in London. It became known as the Russian Flu. It was the most devastating of all influenza epidemics up to this point in recorded history. More than 250,000 people died in Europe, and two to three times that number died worldwide. Eventually the disease struck North America, parts of Africa, and the major Pacific Rim countries. Influenza remained in England with peaks in 1895, 1900, and 1908. The final onslaught was part of the great pandemic of 1918–1919, killing more than 150,000 people.

THE GREAT PANDEMIC

The pandemic that caused more than 20 million deaths struck first in Spain and was called the Spanish Flu. During World War I, the Spanish Flu affected millions. However, even though the numbers of those dying from the flu seemed high, these numbers were overshadowed by what was happening in the war zones. The war effort was hindered on both sides as more and more troops became too ill to fight. For a while the flu appeared to be dormant in the United States, however.

Throughout Europe, the flu acquired a variety of names. In Germany it was called *Blitz Katarrh*, in England and France, *Flanders grippe*, and in Japan it was "wrestler's fever." The spring wave of flu was relatively mild in Spain, England, Japan, and China. Other regions of the world had few, if any, cases. South America was missed completely. The flu had also been spread to the European battlefields by more than 1.5 million American soldiers who crossed the Atlantic to help fight the war. Some died at sea from the disease, while others carried the disease to the front lines and trenches. As the war came to a close, soldiers came home and brought with them a new, more virulent form of the disease.

In the United States, on March 11, 1918, the company cook at Camp Funston (part of Fort Riley), Kansas, reported feeling sick. Albert Gitchell had a fever, sore throat, headache, and muscular aches and pains. As his temperature was being taken, a second soldier, Corporal Lee W. Drake, reported to the same building. His temperature was 103°F, and his symptoms were nearly identical to Gitchell's. By noon, 107 cases had been admitted to the hospital (Figure 9.2). Within a week, 522 cases had been reported in California, Florida, Virginia, Alabama, South Carolina, and Georgia. Persons aboard ships in East Coast harbors and prisoners in San Quentin Prison were also affected.

The second wave of the flu was particularly lethal. As the virus passed through multiple human hosts, it changed from a relatively mild form to something horrible. It reached China in July, Iran early in August, and France in mid-August. When the second wave ended, between 22 and 40 million people were dead worldwide. The actual number will probably never be known. In the United States, 500,000 to 600,000 people died. The disease covered the globe in less than 2 months. How it traveled such great distances in such a short period of time is

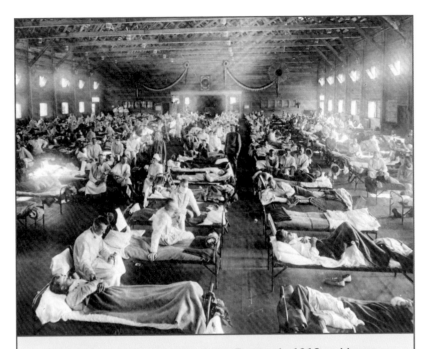

Figure 9.2 Influenza struck Camp Funston in 1918 and began an epidemic that stretched across the United States. Medical personnel at Camp Funston set up an emergency hospital, shown here, to deal with the overwhelming number of flu patients. The virus mutated as it passed among people, and by the time the epidemic ended, more than 500,000 people in the United States had died. (© AP Images)

still unknown. This disease was so widespread that even remote Eskimo villages were completely wiped out. Entrance to the United States probably occurred on August 28, 1918, just outside of Boston. It has been suggested that a sailor on a transport ship in Boston Harbor had symptoms of influenza. By August 30, over 60 sailors were reported ill. Flu sufferers described feeling like they "had been beaten all over with a club." Some of the sailors on this ship were transferred to Michigan and Illinois and became the starting point for the spread of the disease into the Midwest.

Camp Devans, the army base outside Boston, was a supply and exchange point for soldiers going to and coming back from the war. A case of influenza was diagnosed at Camp Devans on September 12. By the end of October, more than 17,000 cases had been reported at Devans. Nearly 800 men in the prime of their lives died. It was said that "dead bodies were stacked in the morgue like cordwood." The disease moved down the East Coast, with death rates ranging from 6 to 15 percent of those affected. In crowded army camps as many as 24,000 soldiers died. By the third week of October, the disease had reached the West Coast and affected all of the major urban areas along the way. The civilian population showed an infection rate of about 28 percent. Often, people attending open-air rallies for the Liberty Loan drives or watching parades of returning soldiers were surrounded by sneezers and coughers.

In Philadelphia 200,000 people gathered at a rally to support the war effort. Within a few days influenza covered the city. Six hundred thirty-five new cases of influenza were reported. The city closed theaters, schools, and churches and passed laws preventing outdoor group meetings. People were required to wear gauze masks when in public. Unfortunately, the gauze was porous and did not stop the virus from escaping into the surroundings. The numbers of cases were staggering in the big cities: 851 New Yorkers died in a 24-hour period. In Boston the number was 202 dead in a day, while in Philadelphia 289 died of the disease in one day. October 1918 was the deadliest month in American history. Philadelphia lost nearly 13,000 of its citizens. A total of nearly 195,000 American citizens died from influenza-related causes that October. The disease became so commonplace that young girls even sang a song as they played and jumped rope:

I had a little bird
Its name was Enza.
I opened the window,
And In-flu-enza

The disease continued to circle the globe. It was estimated that more than 12 million died in India. In some Pacific Islands, mortality figures reached 20 percent of the total population. People living in areas of the world that had not previously experienced respiratory diseases of this type had no built-up immunity. They were extremely susceptible to the ravages of the disease. The more susceptible the population, the higher the mortality rate. The more densely packed the population, the higher the mortality. It was therefore not unusual for urban areas and overcrowded villages to see a large number of deaths.

The disease began a slow retreat in November 1918. Thirty thousand people in San Francisco celebrated the end of the war on November 11 by wearing masks. On November 21, the sirens sounded telling people in San Francisco that it was safe to remove their masks. Thanksgiving Day took on new meaning for some in the United States. In December 5,000 people in San Francisco came down with the flu. In San Diego a general quarantine and the required use of gauze masks occurred that December. (Figure 9.3) The citizens of San Diego had their own little tune.

Obey the laws
And wear the gauze.
Protect your jaws
From septic paws.

The mask law was not popular. Men cut holes in the mask to smoke cigars and cigarettes. Women draped the mask like a veil. Failure to obey the law could result in a $100 fine and 30 days in jail. However, the law was rarely enforced. It has been suggested many times that during the time of the second wave of the flu epidemic in the United States, more people died in America from the flu than in combat in all of the wars of this century.

The postwar years were relatively quiet from a flu stand-point. Regional epidemics continued to flare up, but there was no worldwide pandemic. Research on viruses continued to expand and become more sophisticated. By the 1930s, researchers were looking for an animal host in which to test the disease. In 1932, the structure of the virus was seen with an electron microscope. Three English scientists used throat materials taken from patients, during the epidemic of 1932–1933 in England, to try to infect laboratory animals. The usual laboratory animals of rabbits, mice, and guinea pigs were not affected. Only ferrets showed the symptoms of influenza. By 1940, chicken embryos had become the standard experimental animals. In 1935, Wendell Meredith Stanley showed that viruses consisted of protein and nucleic acid and could be crystallized.

FUTURE CONCERNS

Stephen Spender, an early twentieth century poet, once suggested that "history is the ship carrying living memories into the future." Few are alive today to provide those living memories of the time when influenza was a major regulator of the global population. Our look to the future will conclude by identifying some concerns regarding influenza. It must also be understood that concerns about influenza are part of a larger, more general concern about the emergence of deadly infectious diseases of all types.

In 2002, the State of Minnesota proposed the development of a new Public Health Laboratory Facility. As part of its justification, it has enumerated a number of emerging health concerns that will increase the demand for future laboratory services. That list of concerns is shown here; it clearly demonstrates our common health concerns.

- Increased international travel, making it easier for diseases like tuberculosis or pandemic influenza to spread from one part of the world to another.

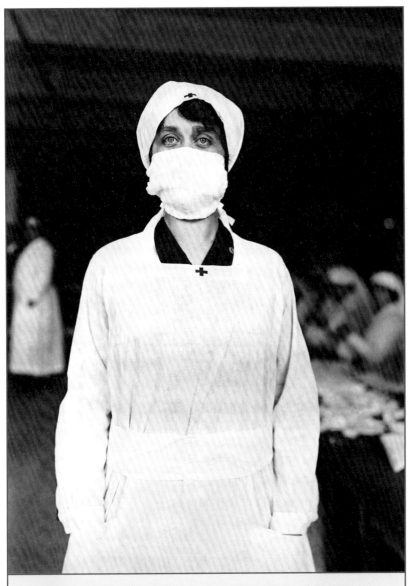

Figure 9.3 Some cities, such as San Francisco and San Diego, California, required citizens to wear masks. However, some people refused to wear the masks, cut holes in them for cigarettes, or wore them like veils instead of masks. In addition, the masks were ineffective anyway because the gauze was porous and the virus could pass through the tiny holes. (© Bettmann/Corbis)

- The globalization of our food supply, potentially exposing us to new foodborne illnesses from other parts of the world.

- Human encroachment on wilderness areas, which increases human exposure to animal species that may harbor new or unusual threats—like hantavirus or the West Nile virus.

- An increase in the number of disease-causing microbes that won't respond to antibiotic treatment.

- Growing concern about the presence in our drinking water of pharmaceuticals and other commercial chemicals, many of which are capable of disrupting the endocrine system or otherwise affecting human health.

- The very real threat of a bioterrorism attack, involving potentially deadly agents like anthrax, smallpox, or plague.
  —Minnesota Department of Health, "Proposed Public Health Lab Facility," February 5, 2002.

It should be clear that our greatest concern is the possibility of another pandemic of the magnitude of the Great Pandemic of 1918. With our increased mobility by land, sea, and air, the entire world could be involved in less than a week. The American College of Physicians has issued several recommendations to consider in preparing for the possibility of the next influenza pandemic. These five recommendations indicate that pandemic preparedness requires the following:[1]

1. Rapidly recognize new virus strains.

2. Establish an adequate surveillance network to detect new strains and assess their effects on populations.

3. Identify the origin of new strains from the animal population.

4. Define the target groups for vaccination.

5. Clarify the role of antiviral drugs.

Many of these recommendations are being actively pursued. The World Health Organization has identified a global agenda for pandemic planning and its influenza surveillance network. However, Dr. Robert Webster, director of the World Health Organization Collaborating Center on the Ecology of Influenza Viruses in Lower Animals and Birds, cites a number of defects and crises associated with these programs. Dr. Webster is concerned that there will be inadequate communication between laboratories working on the ecology of influenza viruses in animals and the surveillance network for human influenza. The 1997 bird flu incident in Hong Kong showed the potential for pandemic infection by transmission from lower animals to humans.

In April 2002, the Agriculture, Fisheries and Conservation Department of Hong Kong indicated that they would begin carrying out dual preventative measures to counteract the possible spread of influenza viruses from chickens to humans. They are depopulating chicken farms in some areas and using a vaccine in other areas. All chicken farms in Hong Kong are under constant monitoring. Dr. Liu Kwei-kin, Deputy Director of the department, stated that:

> We will implement the following three measures at farm level: to amend licensing conditions so as to introduce biosecurity measures and raise hygiene levels on farms; to continue active monitoring of the health of chickens to ensure that only chickens that pass our test can be sold at market; to close any farm concerned once there is an outbreak.[2]

Chickens are not the only animals that can carry influenza viruses. Birds of various types are responsible for transmitting viruses to other animals. Waterfowl do not develop flu symptoms, yet they carry nearly all the known types of influenza viruses. Animals come into contact with the viruses through the fecal materials of the birds. Until the outbreak of flu in Hong Kong in 1997, it was felt that humans could not get the viruses directly from birds. The most common means of transmission from animals to humans was, and is, by way of pigs. As the populations of chickens and pigs has increased through commercial farming, the chances for viral transmission and reassortment within different species have increased.

Dr. Webster's second major concern is the lack of recommendations for stockpiling anti-influenza drugs to deal with a pandemic. There continue to be insufficient supplies of flu vaccine worldwide. The Centers for Disease Control and Prevention estimates it would take about 22 weeks to develop and manufacture a new vaccine. If the cause of the flu pandemic is a viral strain already known, the time might be reduced to 12 weeks. Getting the flu vaccine to the public and overcoming public apathy regarding the severity of the problem are two other concerns.

The final group of concerns to be noted here involves antiviral drugs for use against influenza. There are currently no new antiviral influenza drugs that are being considered.

Most of the public is aware that some bacteria have become resistant to certain antibiotics. While they may not know the cause of the resistance, they have an understanding that this is a significant health care problem. A much smaller percentage of the population realizes that antibiotics cannot be used to treat viruses. What is known by still fewer is that resistance to various influenza, fighting drugs is increasing worldwide. A 2005 study, cited in the journal *The Lancet*, described the results of work done by the CDC, which involved more than 7,000 influenza A isolates. The results indicated that resistance to amantadine and rimantadine had increased by more than 10 percent since the mid-1990s. More than 60 percent of the resistant viruses were isolated from patients in Asia, with some Asian countries showing drug resistance over 70 percent.[3]

The January 17, 2006, issue of *Morbidity and Mortality Weekly Report* (MMWR) reported that 90 percent of the most common causes of influenza A (H3N2) were resistant to amantadine and rimantadine.[4] The CDC recommended that these drugs should not be used to treat the flu during the 2005–2006 flu season. These recommendations refer to human influenza viruses and not the avian influenza (H5N1) that can be isolated from bird or human patients in Asia or Europe, which can also be resistant to these drugs.

The significance of the reports involves the implications of stockpiling these drugs for epidemic and pandemic outbreaks. It appears these drugs can no longer be considered effective for treatment or prevention of influenza outbreaks.

Current antiviral medications fall into two categories. Amantadine (Symmetrel) and rimantadine (Flumavine) are examples of adamantanes or M2 ion channel inhibitors. These chemicals prevent the influenza virus from replicating by blocking the opening of this ion channel formed from the M2 protein. These chemicals are effective only against influenza A viruses and could be used for both prevention and treatment of influenza A viruses, if there is no resistance.[5]

The second group of antiviral medications is the neuraminidase inhibitors, which include oseltamivir (known as Tamiflu) and zanamivir (Relenza). These drugs should be taken between 36 and 48 hours after the start of influenza symptoms. Their job is to slow down the replication of the virus, thus giving the patient's immune system an opportunity to destroy the flu viruses. Their usefulness lies in their ability to decrease the length and severity of the disease conditions. Neuraminidase inhibitors are designed to block the portion of the neuraminidase enzyme that allows it to do its work. This portion of the enzyme is blocked by a synthetic molecule called sialic acid, which mimics the actual sialic acid molecule, the receptor molecule for the viruses' hemagglutinin.

This second group (the neuraminidase inhibitors) works against influenza A and influenza B viruses. Zanamivir is not approved for preventative treatment in the United States. Resistance to the neuraminidase inhibitors is also increasing but is still at lower levels than resistance to amantadine and riamantadine. On December 21, 2005, the FDA extended the use of oseltamivir to include children under 12 years of age. It had previously been limited to children older than 13 years of age.

With its approval the FDA also required that new safety language be added to the label. The safety information suggested that patients stop taking the drug and contact their health care providers if they began to develop a severe skin rash or development of allergic symptoms.[6]

Concern about abnormal behaviors associated with children and adolescents taking oseltamivir led the FDA, in November of 2006, to add safety information regarding neuropsychiatric events. By 2007, reports from Japan indicated that since 2005, 54 people had died after taking oseltamivir. There was concern that the drug might increase the risk for self-injury and delirium in children. There is no evidence to show a link between taking oseltamivir and the deaths. In the United States the Pediatric Advisory Committee of the FDA had confirmed the safety of oseltamivir in 2005, but recommend ongoing surveillance and caution.

In January 2008 the World Health Organization indicated it was carrying out a review of a study showing high levels of resistance to oseltamivir in parts of Europe. A survey of samples from 10 European countries showed about 15 percent resistance to oseltamivir while studies from Norway showed nearly 75 percent resistance. Resistance of the drug to seasonal viral strains is normally from zero to 2 percent.

10

The Future:
Hopes and Dreams

We have come a long way in trying to find ways to treat and cure diseases.
Early attempts to kill microbes were based on uncritical human observations and ranged from the use of moldy bread to whisky, vinegar mixed with egg whites, or gunpowder. Treating materials with heat resulted in developments such as pasteurization, while spraying the operating room with phenol provided an early means of disinfection. Discovery and development of antibiotic chemicals and antibacterial or antimicrobial drugs in the 1930s led to a growing new pharmaceutical industry toward the end of World War II. Killing bacteria, however, has turned out to be a lot easier than destroying viruses.

Viruses are intracellular parasites that use the resources of the host cell to make more viruses. Finding or developing drugs that will destroy or inactivate the viruses without harming the host is a major challenge. Some new antiviral drugs have been developed; however, current research and development for new antivirals is agonizingly slow. Just when scientists think they have finally figured out the latest viral wrinkle, the virus mutates. Where will the future lead us as we attempt to find new treatments for influenza? The February 2008 update from the CDC continued to recommend vaccination with the trivalent influenza vaccines as the most effective method of preventing influenza and the potentially severe complications associated with the disease.[1]

The major problem with these vaccines is that they must be reformulated and administered each year. This is the only way that researchers can deal with the continual mutation of the external viral structure. The World Health Organization decides in February of each year which strains of virus will be part of the new vaccine preparation.

The Flanders Institute for Biotechnology and Ghent University in Belgium have produced a vaccine that is currently being tested by the British-American biotech company Acambis. Dubbed a universal influenza vaccine and known as ACAM-FLU-A, it is being tested on humans in Phase I trials. Phase I trials are designed to determine the safety of a drug and determine the impact of the drug on the human immune system. It is hoped that this universal vaccine would replace the yearly vaccinations and provide protection against all A strains of influenza. The goal is for two inoculations to provide lifelong protection against all of the A strains.

This new vaccine could be made at any time during the year. Because the new vaccine would overcome the constant problem of having to deal with annual mutations, the vaccine could be stockpiled as an advance protection against a possible bird flu outbreak. The vaccine focuses on the M2 protein, which is found on the surface of all strains of type A influenza. This protein, which seems to mutate more slowly than some of the other influenza proteins, is the focus of the current neuraminidase inhibitors such as oseltamivir.

INCREDIBLE EDIBLES

We can all remember being told at some point in our lives: "You are what you eat!" Maybe it was a biology teacher or perhaps a frustrated parent talking to an adolescent who was eating non-stop. Within a few years we may be able to put a new spin on that idea. We now have the technology to genetically engineer plant crops, such as corn, to secrete human antibodies. After a number of unsuccessful attempts, we now have "plantibodies" that are being used to treat non-Hodgkins lymphoma in test animals. Soybeans are being grown with plantibodies against the herpes simplex 2 virus. Epicyte, a biotech company in San Diego, will be starting **clinical trials** of antibody production against herpes simplex 2 using corn kernels. Tobacco plants are producing plantibodies to prevent tooth decay. Proper eating for better health takes on a whole new meaning.

While there is no current edible vaccine for influenza, potatoes are being used as vaccine vehicles for a diabetes vaccine that has been successful in mice. In April 2002, researchers in California identified genes in tomatoes that would enable the tomatoes to be used for production of antibodies against diseases such as cholera. Given the aversion of children and adults to needles, new delivery systems using plants and vegetables would encourage many more people to become vaccinated.

Dr. Hoong-Yeet Yeang of the Rubber Research Institute of Malaysia announced in February 2001 that he had succeeded in producing antibodies against bacteria in the sap of the rubber tree. He also has produced human serum albumin in his rubber trees. This serum albumin is a vital fluid given to patients who are fed intravenously in intensive care units.

THE PATCH

Another type of needle-free vaccine under development is the transcutaneous patch. Dr. De-chu Tang (Figure 10.1), a researcher at the University of Alabama, has developed a needle-free vaccine for influenza that can be swabbed on the skin and covered temporarily with an adhesive patch. Eventually, the vaccine could be incorporated directly into the patch. Trials of the patch are awaiting approval from the Food and Drug Administration (FDA). Five to 10 years of development would follow successful field testing. Mark R. Prausnitz, engineering professor at the Georgia Institute of Technology and his colleagues have developed a tiny patch with 400 needles that poke beneath the upper layers of the skin but above the nerve endings. Figures 10.2 and 10.3 show the overall size of the patch and a magnified view of the needle array. The skin is filled with

Figure 10.1 Dr. De-chu Tang of the University if Alabama is developing a needle-free version of the influenza vaccine. This new vaccine would be applied to the fingertip in liquid form. The skin contains a large number of immune cells; administering the vaccine this way would probably boost the immune response. (Courtesy of Dr. De-chu Tang)

immune cells that provide a useful environment for stimulating the immune system. This improved immune response is another powerful stimulus to development of this method of vaccination. The ability of the patient to self-administer the patch and to obtain the vaccine over the counter at the local pharmacy would increase appeal and efficiency.

THE "HYPOSPRAY"

Those who remember the various *Star Trek* series will recall that the doctors were able to give patients shots directly into

Figure 10.2 Mark Prausnitz and his team at the Georgia Institute of Technology have also developed an alternative influenza vaccine. A tiny patch containing 400 microscopic needles would deliver the vaccine below the skin. This picture shows the size of the patch relative to the patient's finger. (© Gary Meek/Georgia Institute of Technology)

the skin using a painless spraygun called a hypospray. Liquid jet injections have been used for a number of years, particularly by the armed services, with so-called guns that are still often painful. A new system being tested uses helium to push tiny amounts of powdered vaccine into the skin without pain. Developed by a company called PowderJect, this system may be very effective for vaccines because it delivers to the outer layer of the skin. Currently, the company is testing a vaccine against hepatitis B, and the results have shown the vaccine to be both safe and to provide a high degree of immunologic protection. The influenza vaccine is one of those that will be tested with this system. The PowderJect company is also working on a DNA-based influenza vaccine that may provide protection

Figure 10.3 A magnified view of the vaccine patch shows the microscopic needles that would deliver the vaccine underneath the skin. This patch raises the possibility of over-the-counter availability and patient self-administration, making the flu vaccine more accessible to the public. (© Gary Meek/Georgia Institute of Technology)

against antigenic drift. Several studies over the last few years targeting older adults and college students have shown that a short period of muscle-building exercises before receiving a flu shot can improve the person's immune response to the vaccine. While there are gender differences in the impact of the exercise on various aspects of the immune response, it is clear that exercise plays a major role in dealing with the stress associated with receiving the vaccine.[2,3]

NASAL SPRAYS—NOW

FluMist became the first vaccine of any kind to be delivered as a nasal spray. Patient trials have found the vaccine to be highly effective, especially for children. This type of vaccine

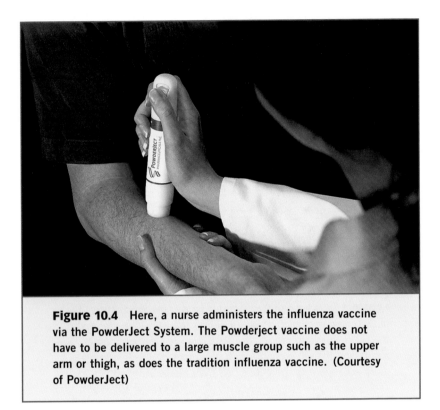

Figure 10.4 Here, a nurse administers the influenza vaccine via the PowderJect System. The Powderject vaccine does not have to be delivered to a large muscle group such as the upper arm or thigh, as does the tradition influenza vaccine. (Courtesy of PowderJect)

offers doctors another tool in their arsenal and helps to make up for shortages of the flu vaccine that have occurred in recent years.

The original research that culminated in the development of FluMist started over 40 years ago. Scientists at the University of Michigan were researching new flu vaccines in the wake of the 1958 pandemic that killed about 70,000 Americans. In 1967 Dr. John Maassab developed a live, "cold-adapted" influenza virus that only grew at the cooler temperatures found in the nasal passages. This characteristic of the virus could prevent infection of the lower respiratory tract, such as the lungs, where the disease normally progresses. The virus was modified so that it could still stimulate an immune response without causing illness. In the 1970s and 1980s, the National Institutes of Health (NIH) took over development of the vaccine and sponsored the patient trials to test the safety, effectiveness, and dosage requirements of the vaccine. In 1995, a private company licensed the vaccine from the university and funded the large clinical trials. The studies involved approximately 24,000 patients and were found to provide protection for more than 90 percent of the patients. The vaccine was also effective in preventing flu-related ear infections. Another advantage of this type of vaccine is that it stimulates a broader range of antibody production. Being administered at the site of the infection stimulates local, humoral (blood-based), and cellular immunity responses. Various United States medical advisory groups have advocated the use of FluMist (nasal spray vaccine) for children between 6 months and 5 years of age. In a multiyear, double-blind study reported in the February 15, 2007, issue of the *New England Journal of Medicine* nearly 8,000 children were tested with either FluMist or an inactivated form of the virus vaccine (the standard shot in the arm version). The study involved children from the United States, Europe, the Middle East, and Asia.

In all cases the group receiving FluMist had about 55 percent fewer cases of flu. While the traditional inactivated viral flu shot causes formation of antibodies in the bloodstream, the FluMist nasal sprays seems to initiate additional antibody response in the nose. Additionally, the immune response in the bloodstream of those taking FluMist also seems to be enhanced. The study group concluded that FluMist should be safe and very effective for children 6 months to 5 years of age who have no history of asthma or wheezing. Children younger than 12 months of age tended to have more cases of wheezing in the second to fourth week after receiving FluMist. Another unintended consequence of the trials showed that patients who had received the FluMist had significantly fewer ear infections which can be a severe complication of the flu.[4]

NASAL SPRAYS—UPDATE

Another nasal spray influenza vaccine currently enrolling subjects into Phase III clinical trials has the brand name FluINsure. In 2005 the company producing FluINsure was approved to begin the first pediatric clinical study of the vaccine at three centers in Canada. Phase III clinical trials were continuing in 2008. There are some significant differences between FluINsure and FluMist. First, FluMist uses a live virus preparation, while FluINsure is a **subunit vaccine** that contains no live viruses. FluINsure is a protein-based nasal vaccine that is not infectious and thus cannot be transmitted from person to person. There are also no interactions with wild type viruses that might be present in the nasal passages of the patient. The preparation of influenza proteins used in the FluINsure vaccine includes the hemagglutinin (HA) protein that has been shown to be important in determining future pandemic strains. There are, according to the company developing FluINsure (ID Biochemical), significant differences in the immune response that is elicited. According to the company, these differences suggest that FluINsure may be superior to FluMist. Only time will tell whether FluINsure is approved for use and if it outperforms FluMist.

LEARNING TO PREDICT
FUTURE INFLUENZA OUTBREAKS

An extremely useful bit of information about influenza would be to know ahead of time what type of influenza A virus has the greatest potential for causing the next major pandemic. Professors Walter Fitch and Robin Bush at the University of California, Irvine, believe they may have identified how viral protein mutations lead to new influenza strains. Working with the CDC, the researchers studied the changes that occurred in a common form of influenza from 1986 to 1997. The group constructed a "family tree" of influenza viruses based on this past information. Then, they tested their ability to correctly predict how the virus would mutate and change. The success rate was nearly 82 percent, nine correct in 11 predictions. Fitch's group discovered that mutations occurring in particular parts of a specific envelope protein were the best predictors of new flu strains. The protein in question is the hemagglutinin protein. Future strains of influenza were most likely to appear when there were several amino acid changes in particular regions of the protein. For new epidemics and pandemics to occur, there needs to be a large, susceptible population. Each time a new variation occurs in the influenza virus, the population no longer has an effective immunity against the flu. New mutations of the virus are required if epidemics or pandemics are to occur. Being able to predict in advance the new strains that will develop would greatly aid development of all types of influenza vaccines.

In September 2001 separate studies published in *Science* magazine reported that researchers had found the genetic causes of two of the most deadly influenza viruses: the virus that caused the 1918 Spanish Flu pandemic and the 1997 Hong Kong strain. This information can be used to distinguish quickly between deadly and relatively harmless viruses. A team of researchers from the Australian National University created a computer program that could analyze genes. They discovered that the genes from the 1918 pandemic came from two different sources and then combined to form a supervirulent strain of the flu. For the first time, scientists found that influenza genes could be spliced or recombined in this way.

Researchers are firmly convinced that the strain of influenza virus responsible for the 1918 pandemic originated in pigs. We know that the Hong Kong virus began in chickens and was shown to be the first time that a virus could move directly from chickens and infect humans. Over one million chickens were killed in Hong Kong in what appears to have been a successful attempt to prevent another epidemic. In June 2002, Protein Sciences Corporation (PSC) announced that it had signed an agreement to produce and distribute a patented

Figure 10.5 Widespread influenza epidemics in Hong Kong have been linked to a strain that had originally infected chickens. Humans contracted the virus by eating infected chickens or having direct contact with the infected animals. In the photo above, workers kill chickens to prevent spreading the avian flu. (© AP Images)

swine flu vaccine internationally. The vaccine is a hemagglutinin vaccine produced through recombinant (gene splicing) technology. In 1997, PSC was awarded the contract to produce a human vaccine in response to the Hong Kong episode. It has worked well in all tests. PSC also has developed recombinant hemagglutinin and recombinant neuraminidase vaccines for human use. These vaccines have proceeded through Phase II clinical trials. Phase III clinical trials will probably begin before the end of 2008.

ADDITIONAL ITEMS OF INTEREST

In June 2002 European authorities approved the use of Tamiflu for the treatment of influenza in adults and children and the prevention of the flu in adolescents and children. Tamiflu has been available in the United States since 1999, when the FDA approved it. It is effective when used within the first 2 days of symptoms and shortens the length of the illness. New laboratory studies are helping to clarify the reasons why those who take Tamiflu are less likely to develop severe complications, such as pneumonia.

A recent breakthrough in the control and spread of infectious diseases, including influenza, was announced in March of 2002 by the Environmental Protection Agency (EPA). Alistagen Corporation, a biotechnology company based in New York City, received approval to market a new antimicrobial surface coating. Called Caliwel, this nontoxic, natural, mineral-based material has been shown to be 99.9 percent effective against more than 20 microbes that cause disease, including influenza. The list includes both bacterial and viral causes. The active ingredient is an encapsulated form of calcium hydroxide. Most airborne microbes are destroyed soon after contact with the coated surface.

Originally, Caliwel was developed with the thought of being used in hospitals, nursing homes, and daycare centers. It can be applied to any hard surface, including floors and walls. It comes in a variety of colors, kills bacteria, fungi, molds, and viruses within minutes and prevents growth on these surfaces for 6 years.

While viruses such as the influenza viruses will continue to represent a constant public health challenge and concern, it should be clear that human ingenuity and creativity are up to the challenge. In this type of battle, the winner has little time to gloat, since the losers are finding new ways to circumvent the previous defenses. There is no ending to this drama, but there is a great challenge that awaits those who are ready to take it on.

It should be clear to all that vaccines will continue to play a vital role in public health on a global scale. Many experts have suggested that the key to public health in the future is directly tied to the development and use of vaccines.[6] In turn, the future of public health is intimately linked to the health and well-being of the world's population. Vaccines have eradicated or reduced diseases such as smallpox, polio, measles, and diphtheria in the developed world.

However, there are scientific, philosophical, and potentially legal challenges in the future development and use of vaccines. Research and development time may be 15 to 25 years for new vaccines. A growing number of parents are using legal exemptions to keep their children from receiving routine immunizations. This type of selective vaccination of children allows deadly infectious diseases to re-enter communities and spread disease. Against this background we need to remember that there are new technologies and breakthroughs that hold the promise of saving millions of young lives now and in the future. We must do everything we can to make sure that all who have a stake in the future of disease prevention and eradication continue to keep talking to each other as if all of our lives depended upon it. Wash your hands. Close the windows. Don't let Enza in.

Notes

Chapter 1

1. W.J. Alonso, C. Viboud, L. Simonsen, E.W. Hirano, L.Z. Daufenbach, and M.A. Miller, "Seasonality of Influenza in Brazil: a Traveling Wave from the Amazon to the Subtropics," *American Journal of Epidemiology* 165, 12 (2007): 1434–1442.

Chapter 2

1. A. Harris, G. Cardone, D.C. Winkler, J.B. Heymann, M. Brecher, J.M. White, and A.C. Steven, "Influenza Virus Pleiomorphy Characterized by Cryoelectron Tomography," *Proceedings—National Academy of Sciences USA* 103, 50 (2006): 19123–19127, http://www.pnas.org/cgi/content/full/103/50/19123, (accessed May 28, 2008).

2. U.S. Department of Health and Human Services, "NIAID Launches Influenza Genome Sequencing Project," *NIH News*, November 15, 2004, http://www.nih.gov/news/pr/nov2004/niaid-15.htm, (accessed May 28, 2008).

3. E. Ghedin, N.A. Sengamalay, M. Shumway, J. Zaborsky, T. Feldblyum, V. Subbu, D.J. Spiro, J. Sitz, H. Koo, and P. Bolotov, "Large-Scale Sequencing of Human Influenza Reveals the Dynamic Nature of Viral Genome Evolution," *Nature* 7062 (2005): 1162–1166.

4. Infection Control Today, "2,000 Influenza Virus Genomes Now Completed and Publicly Accessible," *ICT Magazine*, February 21, 2007, http://www.infectioncontroltoday.com/hotnews/72h2114302117346.html, (accessed May 28, 2008).

5. A.C. Lowen, S. Mubareka, J. Steel, and P. Palese, "Influenza Virus Transmission Is Dependent on Relative Humidity and Temperature," *Public Library of Science Pathogens* 3, 10 (2007): 1470–1476.

6. I.V. Polozov, L. Bezrukov, K. Gawrisch and J. Zimmerberg, "Progressive ordering with decreasing temperature of the phospholipids of influenza virus," *Nature Chemical Biology* 4 (2008): 248–255.

7. U.S. Food and Drug Administration, "Influenza Virus Vaccine 2008–2009 Season," http://www.fda.gov/cber/flu/flu2008.htm, (accessed May 28, 2008).

Chapter 3

1. T. Noda, H. Sagara, A. Yen, A. Takada, H. Kida, R. H. Cheng, and Y. Kawaoka, "Architecture of Ribonucleoprotein Complexes in Influenza A Virus Particles," *Nature* 7075 (2006): 490–492.

Chapter 4

1. P.J. Allen, "Home Care Fact Sheet for Influenza," *Pediatric Nursing* 32, 6 (2006): 573–578.

Chapter 5

1. Howard Hughes Medical Institute, "Immunology: Virtual Lab," http://www.hhmi.org/biointeractive/immunology/vlab.html, (accessed April 10, 2008).

Chapter 6

1. J.S. Brownstein, K.P. Kleinman, and K.D. Mandl, "Identifying Pediatric Age Groups for Influenza Vaccination Using a Real-Time Regional Surveillance System," *American Journal of Epidemiology* 162, 7 (2005): 686–693.

2. D.M. Zerr, J.A. Englund, A.S. Robertson, E.K. Marcuse, M.M. Garrison, and D.A. Christakis, "Hospital-Based Influenza Vaccination of Children: An Opportunity to Prevent Subsequent Hospitalization," *Pediatrics—Springfield* 121, 2 (2008): 345–348.

3. Medical News Today, "Starting Flu Vaccination In August Could Help Protect Nearly 11 Million More Children During Scheduled Doctors' Visits," May 6, 2008, http://www.medicalnewstoday.com/articles/106347.php, (accessed May 27, 2008).

4. American Academy of Pediatrics Committee on Infectious Diseases, "Prevention of Influenza: Recommendations for Influenza Immunization of Children, 2007–2008," *Pediatrics* 121, 4 (2008): 1016–1031.

Notes

5. Medical News Today, "National Foundation For Infectious Diseases Urges Increased Influenza Vaccination Rates For Persons With Diabetes," February 22, 2007, http://www.medicalnewstoday.com/articles/63589.php, (accessed May 27, 2008).

6. K.H. Ellis, "CDC releases pandemic flu preparedness plans," *Infectious Disease News*, March 2007, http://www.infectiousdiseasenews.com/200703/pandemic.asp, (accessed May 27, 2008).

Chapter 7

1. K. Takabayshi, M. Corr, T. Hayashi, V. Redecke, L. Beck, D. Guiney, D. Sheppard, and E. Raz, "Induction of a Homeostatic Circuit in Lung Tissue by Microbial Compounds," *Immunity* 24, 4 (2006): 475–487.

2. J. Wrammert, *et al.* "Rapid cloning of high-affinity human monoclonal antibodies against influenza virus," *Nature* 453, 7195 (2008): 667, http://www.nature.com/nature/journal/vaop/ncurrent/full/nature06890.html, (accessed June 26, 2008).

3. A. Elliot, and J. Ellis. "Influenza Prevention and Treatment - an Update," *Pharmaceutical Journal* 265, 7115 (2000): 446–450.

Chapter 8

1. World Health Organization Global Influenza Program Surveillance Network, "Evolution of H5N1 Avian Influenza Viruses in Asia," *Emerging Infectious Diseases* 11, 10 (2005): 1515–1521.

2. B. Olsen, "Global Patterns of Influenza A Virus in Wild Birds," *Science* 312, 5772 (2006): 384–388.

3. A. Trafton, "MIT finds key to avian flu in humans," *MIT News*, January 6, 2008, http://web.mit.edu/newsoffice/2008/bird-flu-0106.html, Accessed May 28, 2008.

4. E.W. Rice, "Chlorine Inactivation of Highly Pathogenic Avian Influenza (H5N1)," *Emerging Infectious Diseases* 13, 10 (2007): 1568–1570, http://www.cdc.gov/EID/content/13/10/1568.htm. Accessed May 28, 2008.

Chapter 9

1. P. Gross. "Preparing for the Next Influenza Pandemic: A Reemerging Infection," *Annals of Internal Medicine* 124, 7 (1996): 682–685, http://www.annals.org/cgi/content/full/124/7/682, (accessed June 26, 2008).

2. Hong Kong government Web site, "Measures to control chicken flu in Pak Sha," April 6, 2002, http://www.info.gov.hk/gia/general/200204/06/0406176.htm (accessed May 27, 2008).

3. R.A. Bright, M.J. Medina, X. Xu, G. Perez-Oronoz, T.R. Wallis, X.M. Davis, L. Povinelli, N.J. Cox, and A.I. Klimov, "Incidence of Adamantane Resistance Among Influenza A (H3N2) Viruses Isolated Worldwide from 1994 to 2005: a Cause for Concern," *Lancet* 366, 9492 (2005): 1175–1181.

4. Centers for Disease Control and Prevention, "Update: Influenza Activity—United States, January 1–7, 2006," *MMWR Morbidity and Mortality Weekly Report* 55, 2 (2006): 46–48.

5. A. Elliot and J. Ellis, "Influenza prevention and treatment—an update," *The Pharmaceutical Journal* 265, 7115 (2000): 446–451, http://www.pharmj.com/Editorial/20000923/special_feature/influenza.html, (accessed May 28, 2008).

6. U.S. Food and Drug Administration, "FDA Approves Tamiflu for Prevention of Influenza in Children Under Age 12," *FDA News*, December 22, 2005, http://www.fda.gov/bbs/topics/news/2005/new01285.html, (accessed May 28, 2008).

Chapter 10

1. Centers for Disease Control and Prevention, "Update: Influenza Activity—United States, September 30, 2007–February 9, 2008," *MMWR Morbidity and Mortality Weekly Report* 57, 7 (2008):179–183.

2. K.M. Edwards, V.E. Burns, L.M. Allen, J.S. McPhee, J.A. Bosch, D. Carroll,

M. Drayson, and C. Ring, "Eccentric Exercise As an Adjuvant to Influenza Vaccination in Humans," *Brain Behavior and Immunity* 21, 2 (2007): 209–217.

3. M.L. Kohut, B.A. Arntson, W. Lee, K. Rozeboom, K.J. Yoon, J.E. Cunnick, and J. McElhaney, "Moderate Exercise Improves Antibody Response to Influenza Immunization in Older Adults," *Vaccine* 22, (2004): 17–18.

4. R.B. Belshe, "Live Attenuated Versus Inactivated Influenza Vaccine in Infants and Young Children," *New England Journal of Medicine* 356, 7 (2007): 685–696.

5. Infection Control Today, "Experts Agree: Vaccines Give Healthcare a Needed Shot in the Arm," *ICT Magazine*, May 15, 2008, http://www.infectioncontroltoday.com/hotnews/vaccines-boost-healthcare.html, (accessed May 27, 2008).

adsorption—The process by which an object sticks to a surface; sometimes used synonymously with attachment when talking about viruses.

AIDS—*Acquired immunodeficiency syndrome*; caused by HIV and character-ized by loss of or diminished immune system function; death may result from diseases such as pneumonia that would ordinarily have been taken care of by a healthy immune system.

antibiotics—Substances usually produced by microbes or fungi that can destroy or inhibit the growth and reproduction of other microorganisms.

antibody—Protein produced by a plasma cell (modified B lymphocyte) in response to the presence and recognition of an antigen; major fighter for the immune system.

antibody-mediated immunity—See humoral immunity.

antigen—A molecule, group of molecules, or part of a cell that is recognized by the host immune cells as being *non-self* or foreign; stimulates production of antibodies (*anti*body *gen*erating).

antiviral—Drugs designed to destroy or prevent the replication of viruses which result in decreased severity or shortened time of disease process.

Asian Flu—Name usually associated with 1957 pandemic that killed over one million people.

B cells or **B lymphocytes**—White blood cells derived from and matured in bone marrow; when stimulated they develop into plasma cells, which pro-duce antibodies.

capsid—Protein outer covering of a virus particle.

capsomeres—Individual protein subunits that make up the capsid.

cell-mediated or **cellular immunity (CMI)**—T lymphocyte and other immune system cells that seek out and attempt to destroy invaders directly, in con-trast to soluble protein antibodies that often tag or identify invaders for other cells to destroy.

clinical trials—Rigorous scientific evaluation of a procedure, device, or drug(s) used for prevention, diagnosis, or treatment of a disease; usually three phases (phases I, II, III) required for approval by the FDA (Food and Drug Administration).

Phase I: Evaluation of clinical pharmacology, involves volunteers; testing for safety.

Phase II: Performed in a small group of patients; testing for dosage and overall desired clinical effect.

Phase III: Large, comparative study using patients to establish a clear clinical benefit; control groups using placebos or comparisons to established or current procedures.

cytokines—General term for chemical substances produced by a variety of cells; lymphokines are one example; effects vary with cell type produced and affected; high concentrations may be toxic; interferon is one type.

cytotoxic T cells—A subpopulation of the T lymphocytes; will find and destroy cells that have been modified by infection with bacteria, fungi, or viruses or by some cancer-producing factor; also known as killer T cells.

drift or **genetic drift**—A gradual change in the structure of one of the proteins in the envelope of the virus, usually the hemagglutinin protein; these genetic changes occur because of the lack of error checking that occurs with RNA viruses when they are copying their genome; will lead to new subtypes that require new vaccine preparations.

endocytosis—The general term for taking other cells, particles, or molecules into the cell; the cell must use energy to accomplish this task; when a cell becomes irritated or stimulated by contact with its membrane, it may engulf the stimulant or irritant; some viruses enter cells in this manner.

envelope—Outermost portion of some viruses; may consist of a portion of the animal cell's membranes and contain unique proteins and lipids.

enzyme—Protein that serves as an organic catalyst; speeds up the rate of a biochemical reaction but is not consumed or used up in that reaction; all biochemical reactions within living systems are controlled or regulated by enzymes.

epidemic—A dramatic increase in the number of individuals showing the symptoms of a disease within a specified area and during a specified time period; in the United States, statistics to determine a true epidemic are collected and maintained by the CDC.

eukaryotic—A eukaryote cell. A eukaryote is an organism whose cells contain a distinct membrane-bound nucleus.

genome—Sum total of all the genetic information in a cell or virus.

helper T cells—A subgroup of T lymphocytes that are the main regulators of immune system responses; involved in many functions including activation of antibody production and activation of cytotoxic T cells.

hemagglutinin (HA)—Protein that is found as part of the outer envelope of the influenza virus; required for attachment and penetration of the virus into the cell; rod-shaped spike; named for its ability to cause agglutination or clumping of red blood cells.

Haemophilus influenzae—Bacterium found in the respiratory tract originally thought to be responsible for the flu; causes secondary infections of the respiratory tract, including pneumonia.

HIV—*Human immunodeficiency virus;* the virus responsible for AIDS.

Hong Kong Flu—Common name for the strain of influenza Type A virus that killed nearly 750,00 people in 1968; another Hong Kong flu emerged in 1997 with six deaths; millions of chickens feared to be the cause of the disease were slaughtered.

humoral immunity—Refers to circulating parts of the immune system, soluble proteins in the gamma globulin fragment of the plasma of the blood, namely, the antibodies.

inflammation—A series of responses consisting of redness, increased heat in the area, swelling, and pain; this is followed by repair of the inflamed area; part of the nonspecific defenses of the body.

influenza—Commonly called the flu; a serious viral disease; infects the respiratory tract; can lead to severe and deadly complications.

interferon—A family of proteins that acts nonselectively in response to the presence of viruses in a cell; serves as an early warning sytem.

intracellular—Within a cell.

lymphocytes—One of the five types of white blood cells produced by humans; divided into B and T lymphocytes that are both essential to proper immune function.

lymphokines—Cyokines produced by lymphocytes; help to regulate action of immune system.

macrophage—A modified version of the monocyte, one of the five types of white blood cells in humans; a large cell that seeks out and engulfs foreign particles and cells through phagocytosis; literally a large eater.

mutation—Change in the genetic information of a cell or virus (either DNA or RNA in some viruses); changes in genetic information usually lead to new proteins, altered proteins, or loss of proteins.

natural killer (NK) cells—Lymphocytes that kill infected cells and tumor cells; they attack without receiving specific chemical messages from the T cells; important in antiviral defenses.

neuraminidase (NA)—Protein that is part of the outer envelope of the influenza virus; serves as an enzyme and is responsible for newly formed viruses escaping the host cells; aids in spread of the virus.

neutrophil—One of the five types of white blood cells in humans; these are the most numerous, making up about 60 percent of the total white blood cells under normal circumstances; highly phagocytic.

nucleocapsids—Viruses that have only a capsid (coat) and genetic material.

organelles—Differentiated structures within a cell, which perform a specific function.

pandemic—Worldwide epidemic; widespread disease in humans; results when person-to-person contact occurs among individuals who have the virus but no current immune protection against it (these types of individuals are sometimes called immunologically naïve).

parasite—An organism or viral particle that invades and lives within another cell or organism (called the host) using the resources of that cell; the parasite benefits from the relationship but the host is harmed or may be killed.

pathogenic—An organism or entity capable of causing disease.

pericarditis—Inflammation of the pericardium, the membrane sac that encloses the heart.

phagocytosis—A type of active transport involving the entire cell; the general term for the cell's using energy to bring cells, particles, or molecules into itself is active transport, and the action taken by the cell is called endocytosis. The cell surrounds and then engulfs its prey; the prey is then enclosed in a membranous structure that will fuse with lysosomes and digest the prey; its molecules will then diffuse into the cell for reuse.

plasma cells—Transformed B lymphocytes that have been stimulated by a specific antigen; they produce millions of copies of a single protein antibody specific for the antigen.

prokaryotic—A prokaryote cell. A prokaryote is a single-celled organism that lacks a distinct, membrane-bound nucleus or membrane-bound organelles, and which has DNA that is not organized into chromosomes.

protists—Single-celled, eukaryotic organisms that often form colonies. This kingdom of organisms includes protozoans, most algae, and some fungi.

reassortment—In the context of this book, it refers to a rearrangement and combination of genes from two different and distinct influenza strains that leads to production of a new or novel influenza strain.

receptor-mediated endocytosis—The act of a cell taking in other cells, particles, or molecules after they have attached themselves to specific protein receptor molecules in the host cell's membrane; the influenza virus enters its host in this way.

replicate—To make an exact copy; the process of duplicating or reproducing as in viral replication.

serology—Study of serum.

seropositive—Individual possessing antibodies specific to a particular strain of virus or bacteria.

serum—The clear light yellow-orange fluid left when the formed elements and the clotting factors of the blood are removed is the serum; the entire liquid portion of the blood is called the plasma and contains the formed elements (red blood cells, white blood cells, and platelets); it also contains a number of soluble proteins, including the antibodies and the clotting factors.

shift or **genetic shift**—Abrupt, major genetic change that produces a novel influenza A subtype that was not currently circulating among humans; this new strain may be the result of reassortment of currently circulating influenza strains or of direct contact between the lower animals and humans; often these new strains lead to epidemics or pandemics.

Spanish Flu—Common name given to the pandemic of 1918–1920; responsible for more than 20 million deaths.

subtype—Among the Influenza Type A viruses, there are currently 15 subtypes or variations within that broader category.

subunit vaccines—A vaccine that uses only one or more of the parts of a disease-causing organism or virus to stimulate an immune reaction.

surveillance—A continuous and organized collection and analysis of data regarding all aspects of influenza; the information is then sent to national and regional public health professionals, who use it to provide an up-to-date prevention and control program.

T cell or **T lymphocyte**—A subpopulation of lymphocytes; they are involved in cell-mediated immunity and are well known in transplant rejection situations; they release a number of different kinds of cytokines; there are four different types of T cells: helper T cells, suppressor T cells, cytotoxic T cells, and delayed hypersensitivity T cells.

transcription—Part of protein synthesis process in which information in DNA molecule is converted into a messenger RNA (mRNA).

type—When used in reference to influenza virus, it is one of three broad categories or classes; there is influenza type A, type B, and type C.

vaccine—A substance, organism, viral particle, or group of molecules that, when injected or put into the body by other means, causes the immune system to provide an immune response to that specific agent; supplied antigens that stimulate production of antibodies.

virion—A complete virus particle consisting of capsid and genome.

virology—The study of viruses.

virus—A submicroscopic, infectious particle consisting of a protein covering called the capsid, which encloses genetic information and the genome; there may be an additional outer envelope; viruses are intracellular parasites.

Bibliography

Chapter 1

ASM News 59, 8 (1993): 402.

Brock, Thomas. *Milestones in Microbiology.* Upper Saddle River, NJ: Prentice-Hall, 1961.

BSCS, Videodiscovery, NIH Curriculum Supplement Series, National Institute of Allergy and Infectious Diseases, *Emerging and Re-emerging Infectious Diseases.* Bethesda, Md.: NIH Publication, October 1999.

Burnett, Sir MacFarlane and David O. White. *Natural History of Infectious Disease,* 4th ed. London: Cambridge University Press, 1972.

General influenza information
http://www.pbs.org/wgbh/amex/influenza

Haimann, Barbara. *Disease: Identification, Prevention, and Control.* St. Louis: Mosby-Year Book Inc., 1994.

Kolata, Gina. *Flu: The Story of the Great Influenza Pandemic of 1918 and the Search for the Virus That Caused It.* New York: Farrar, Straus & Giroux Publishers, 1999.

Madigan, M.T., Martinko, J.M., and J. Parker. *Brock Biology of Microorganisms.* 8th ed. Upper Saddle River, N.J.: Prentice Hall, 1997.

Marks, Geoffrey and William K. Beatty. *Epidemics.* New York: Charles Scribner's Sons, 1976.

McCullough, David. *John Adams.* New York: Simon & Schuster, 2001.

McNeil, William H. *Plagues and Peoples.* Garden City, N.Y.: Doubleday, 1976.

Mims, Cedric A. *The Pathogenesis of Infectious Disease.* San Diego, Calif.: Academic Press, 1977.

Morison, Samuel Eliot. *The Oxford History of the American People.* New York: Oxford University Press, 1965.

MSNBC.com "Influenza's reach over time." *MSNBC.com,* December 17, 1997. Available online. URL: *http://www.msnbc.com/news/130842.asp?cp=1=1.* Accessed September 2, 2008.

San Diego pictures
http://www.sandiegohistory.org/stranger/flu.htm

Table showing death rates
http://www.pbs.org/wgbh/amex/influenza/maps/index.html

Chapter 2

Diagram of structure of HA
http://www.uct.ac.za/depts/mmi/jmoodie/influen2.html

Diagrams showing structure and organization of influenza viruses
http://www-ermm.cbcu.cam.ac.uk/01002460h.htm

Chapter 3

Alcamo, I.E. *Fundamentals of Microbiology,* 6th ed. Sudbury, Mass.: Jones and Bartlett Publishers, 2001.

Goto, Hideo and Yoshihiro Kawaoka. "A novel mechanism for the acquisition of virulence by a human influenza A virus." *Proceedings of the National Academy of Sciences USA* 95 (1998): 10224–10228.

Laver, W. Graeme, Norbert Bischofberger, and Robert G. Webster. "Disarming Flu Viruses." *Scientific American* 280, 1 (January 1999): 78–87.

Lewis, Ricki, "Electron microscopy reveals protein translocation channel." *BioPhotonics News* (Jan.–Feb. 1997).

Madigan, Michael T., John M. Martinko, and Jack Parker. *Brock: Biology of Microorganisms,* 8th ed. Upper Saddle River, N.J.: Prentice Hall, 1997.

Purves, William K., Sadava, David, Orians, Gondanlt, and H. Craig Heller. *Life: The Science of Biology,* 6th ed. Sunderland, Mass.: W.H. Freeman and Co., 2001.

Tortora, Gerard J., Berdell R. Funke, and Christine L. Case. *Microbiology: An Introduction,* 6th ed. Menlo Park, Calif.: Benjamin Cummings Publishing Co., 1998.

Voyles, Bruce A. *The Biology of Viruses.* St. Louis, Mo.: Mosby-Year Book, 1993.

Wagner, Edward K. and Martinez, J. Hewlett. *Basic Virology.* Malden, Mass.: Blackwell Science, Inc., 1999.

Chapter 4

American Lung Association
http://lungusa.org

National Reye's Syndrome Foundation
http://www.reyessyndrome.org

Chapter 5

Alcamo, I.E. *Fundamentals of Microbiology*, 6th ed. Sudbury, Mass.: Jones and Bartlett Publishers, 2001.

Finegold, Sydney M. and William J. Martin. *Diagnostic Microbiology*, 6th ed. St. Louis, Mo.: C.V. Mosby, 1982.

Howard Hughes Medical Institute, Information on Immune System. *http://www.hhmi.org/biointeractive/animations/tcell/tcell_print.htm*

Howard Hughes Medical Institute Virtual Laboratory. *http://www.hhmi.org/biointeractive/vlabs/index.htm*

Koneman E.W., S.D. Allen, V.R. Dowell, Jr., and Herbert M. Sommers. *Color Atlas and Textbook of Diagnostic Microbiology*, 2d ed. Philadelphia: J.B. Lippincott Company, 1983.

Laboratory Diagnostic Procedures for Influenza, National Center for Infectious Diseases. *http://www.cdc.gov/ncidod/diseases/flu*

MEDLINE Plus, Medical Encyclopedia. *http://www.nlm.nih.gov/medlineplus/ency*

Chapter 6

Centers for Disease Control and Prevention. "Prevention and Control of Influenza, Recommendations of the Advisory Committee on Immunization Practices." *Morbidity and Mortality Weekly Report* 51, RR-3 (April 12, 2002).

National Institute of Allergy and Infectious Diseases *http://www.niaid.nih.gov/topics/flu/default.htm*

U.S. Department of Health and Human Services, Public Health Service, Centers for Disease Control and Prevention. "Addressing Emerging Infectious Disease Threats: A Prevention Strategy for the United States." *Morbidity and Mortality Weekly Report* 43 RR-5 (April 15, 1994): 1–18.

U.S. Department of Health and Human Services, National Institute of Allergy and Infectious Diseases. "Understanding Vaccines." NIH Publication No. 98-4219 (January 1998).

World Health Organzation (WHO)
http://www.who.int

Chapter 7

National Institutes of Health, National Institute of Allergy and Infectious Diseases. "Understanding Vaccines." U.S. Department of Health and Human Services, NIH Publication No. 98-4219 (January 1998).

National Institutes of Health, National Institute of Allergy and Infectious Diseases. "Understanding Autoimmune Diseases." U.S. Department of Health and Human Services, NIH Publication No. 98-4273 (May 1998).

Schindler, Lydia Woods. "Understanding the Immune System." U.S. Department of Health and Human Services, Public Health Service, National Institutes of Health, NIH Publication No. 90-529, revised (March 1990).

National Institutes of Health, National Institute of General Medical Sciences. "Medicines By Design: The Biological Revolution in Pharmacology." NIH Publication No. 93-474 (September 1993).

Chapter 9

Gillette, B. "Pork Production is Linked to the Risk of Epidemics and Infections." *E-Magazine* (May-June 2000). Available online. URL: *http://www.organicconsumers.org/toxic/porkfilth.cfm.* Accessed September 2, 2008.

Gross, Peter A. "Preparing for the Next Influenza Pandemic: A Reemerging Infection." *Annals of Internal Medicine, American College of Physicians* 124 (1996): 682-685.

Vaccine Bulletin 156 June 2002, Clinical Update
http://www.vaccinebulletin.com/156/clin156.html

Chapter 10

Ainsworth, Claire. "Antibodies Could be Grown in Fields." *New Scientist,* (October 3, 2001). *http://www.newscientist.com/article/dn1373-antibodies-could-be-grown-in-fields.html.* Accessed September 2, 2008.

Bush, Robin M., Catherine A. Bender, Kata Subbarao, Nancy J. Cox, and Walter M. Fitch. "Predicting the Evolution of Human Influenza A," *Science* 286 (1999): 1924–1925.

Caliwel product information news
http://www.caliwel.com

Coghlan, Andy. "Tree of Life." *New Scientist,* (February 9, 2001). *http://www.newscientist.com/article/dn-407-tree-of-life.html.* Accessed September 2, 2008.

Graeme, Laver and Elspeth Garman, "The Origin and Control of Pandemic Influenza." *Science* 293 (September 7, 2001): 1776–1777.

Masato Hatta, Peng Gao, Peter Halfmann, and Yoshihiro Kawaoka. "Molecular Basis for High Virulence of Hong Kong H5N1 Influenza Viruses." *Science* 293 (September 7, 2001): 1840.

Webster, Robert G. "A Molecular Whodunit." *Science* 293 (September 7, 2001): 1773–1775.

Books and Articles

Ahmad Al-Azemi, et al. "Avian Influenza A Virus (H5N1) Outbreaks, Kuwait, 2007," *Emerging Infectious Diseases*, 14, 6 (June 2008): 958–961. Available online. URL: http://www.cdc.gov/eid/content/14/6/958.htm. Accessed June 16, 2008.

de Jong, M. D. "Brief Report: Oseltamivir Resistance During Treatment of Influenza A (H5N1) Infection," *New England Journal of Medicine*, 353, 25 (2005): 2667–2672.

Hellemans, Alexander. "Beating the Flu in a Single Shot," *Scientific American*, 298, 6 (June 2008): 104. Available online. URL: http://www.sciam.com/article.cfm?id=beating-the-flu. Accessed June 16, 2008.

Nichol, K. L. "Influenza Vaccination and Reduction in Hospitalizations for Cardiac Disease and Stroke Among the Elderly," *New England Journal of Medicine* 348 (2003): 1322–1332.

Normile, Dennis. "Flu Virus Research Yields Results but No Magic Bullet for Pandemic," *Science* 319, 5867 (2008): 1178–1179.

Offit, Paul A. *Vaccinated: One Man's Quest to Defeat the World's Deadliest Diseases.* Washington, D.C.: Smithsonian Books, 2007.

Oshitani, Hitoshi, Kamigaki, Taro and Suzuki, Akira. "Major Issues and Challenges of Influenza Pandemic Preparedness in Developing Countries," *Emerging Infectious Diseases*, 14, 6 (June 2008): 875–880. Available online. URL: http://www.cdc.gov/eid/content/14/6/875.htm. Accessed June 16, 2008.

Peiris, J. S. M. "Re-Emergence of Fatal Human Influenza A Subtype H5N1 Disease," *The Lancet* 9409 (2004): 617–618.

Russell, Colin A, et al. "The Global Circulation of Seasonal Influenza A (H3N2) Viruses," *Science* 320, 5874 (2008): 340.

Ungchusak, K. "Probable Person-to-Person Transmission of Avian Influenza A (H5N1)," *New England Journal of Medicine* 352, 4 (2005): 333–340.

Web Sites

Contagion: Historical Views of Disease and Epidemics
http://ocp.hul.harvard.edu/contagion

Global Wildlife Disease News Map
http://wildlifedisease.nbii.gov/wdinNewsDigestMap.jsp

Further Resources

A Student's Guide to the Medical Literature
http://grinch.uchsc.edu/sg/index.html

USDA: Animal and Plant Health Inspection Service
http://www.aphis.usda.gov

Index

Index

(-)negative-stranded RNA virus, 33

neuraminic acid, 39

neuraminidase (NA)
  and antigenic shift, 98
  and antiviral medications, 47
  and flu virus structure, 16
  and genetic drift, 23
  and H3N2 flu virus, 20
  and monoclonal antibodies, 93
  and subtype naming, 20
  and transmission, 78
  and Type A flu virus, 36
  and viral replication, 39
  ZstatFlu test for, 61

neuraminidase-inhibitor drugs, 39, 114–115

neuropsychiatric events, 115

neutrophil, 84, 85, 90

New England Journal of Medicine, 123

New York City, 107

NFID (National Foundation for Infectious Diseases), 72–73

NIAID (National Institute of Allergy and Infectious Disease), 20–21

NIAMS (National Institute of Arthritis and Musculoskeletal and Skin Disease), 19

NICHD (National Institute of Child Health and Human Development), 24

NIH. *See* National Institutes of Health

1918 Spanish Flu pandemic. *See* Spanish Flu pandemic

NK cells. *See* natural killer cells

NLV (Norwalk-like virus), 49

NMRI (nuclear magnetic resonance imaging), 24

non-pharmaceutical intervention, 77

nonspecific defenses, 84

normal flora, 81

Northern Hemisphere, 73

Norwalk-like virus (NLV), 49

Norwalk virus, 43–44

nuclear magnetic resonance imaging (NMRI), 24

nucleocapsids, 15, 17, 33, 39

nucleoproteins, 17

organelles, 14, 135

Orthomyxoviridae, 33

oseltamivir, 39, 46–47, 69, 101, 114, 115, 126–127

otitis media, 82

Ott, Fred, 68

outbreaks, surveillance of, 75–76

over-the-counter medications, 45, 46

Palese, Peter, 24

pandemics, 16, 76, 102–104, 109–115, 135. *See also specific pandemics, e.g.:* Spanish Flu

parasite, 135

PAS (Pediatric Academic Societies), 65

patch, 118–121

PCR (polymerase chain reaction), 61–62

Pediatric Academic Societies (PAS), 65

Pediatric Advisory Committee, 115

penetration (by virus), 29, 30

pericarditis, 82

Persian Gulf War (1990–1991), 49

personal hygiene, 66

phagocytosis, 84

Philadelphia, Pennsylvania, 107

phospholipid, 15

pigs, as virus reservoirs, 100, 113, 125

plasma, 61

plasma cells, 88, 89

plasmin, 36

plasminogen, 36

platelets, 61

pneumonia, 48, 80–81, 84

pneumonia vaccine, 70

polymerase chain reaction (PCR), 61–62

(+) positive-stranded RNA virus, 32–33

poultry, and H5N1 virus, 94, 96

poultry flu, 48

PowderJect System, 120–122

Prausnitz, Mark R., 118

prediction, of outbreaks, 122–124

prescription drugs, 46–47

preventative medications, 47, 68–69. *See also specific medications, e.g.:* Tamiflu

prevention, 47–50, 63–77, 100–101

prokaryotic cells, 14

protease, 36

protein, 23, 34, 60

protein coat, 18, 96–97

Protein Sciences Corporation, 125–126

protein translocation channels, 37–38

prothrombin, 61

protists, 14, 135

public health, 69, 127–128

Public Health Laboratory Facility (Minnesota), 109, 111

rapid testing, 52–53, 61

Rapoport, Thomas, 37–38

Raz, Eyal, 87

RCA (Recognition, Communication, Action) sequence, 60, 91

reassortment, 20, 25–26, 98

About the Author

Dr. Don Emmeluth spent most of his teaching career in upstate New York. In 1999, Dr. Emmeluth retired from the State University of New York system and moved to Savannah, Georgia. He became a member of the Biology Department of Armstrong Atlantic State University in Savannah, where he teaches a number of courses.

Dr. Emmeluth has published several journal articles and is the co-author of a high school biology textbook. His most recent article appeared in the February 2002 issue of *The American Biology Teacher*. He has also authored three other books in the Deadly Diseases and Epidemics series: *Typhoid Fever, Plague, and Botulism*.

Dr. Emmeluth has served as President of the National Association of Biology Teachers. During his career, Dr. Emmeluth has received a number of honors and awards including the Chancellor's Award for Excellence in Teaching from the State University of New York system and the Two-Year College Biology Teaching Award from NABT. In 2003, Dr. Emmeluth was awarded NABT's Honorary Membership Award for outstanding contributions to Biology and Life Science Education. This award is the association's highest honor.

About the Consulting Editor

Hilary Babcock, M.D., M.P.H., is an Assistant Professor of Medicine at Washington University School of Medicine at Washington University School of Medicine and the Medical Director of Occupational Health for Barnes-Jewish Hospital and St. Louis Children's Hospital. She received her undergraduate degree from Brown University and her M.D. from the University of Texas Southwestern Medical Center at Dallas. After completing her residency, chief residency, and Infectious Disease fellowship at Barnes-Jewish Hospital, she joined the faculty of the infectious disease division. She completed an M.P.H. in Public Health from St. Louis University School of Public Health in 2006. She has lectured, taught, and written extensively about infectious diseases, their treatment, and their prevention. She is a member of numerous medical associations and is board certified in infectious disease. She lives in St. Louis, Missouri.